TK
7885.7
.T48
1991

Thomas, D. E. (Donald
E.), 1951-

The Verilog hardware
description
language.

$55.00

DATE			

THE VERILOG® HARDWARE DESCRIPTION LANGUAGE

THE VERILOG® HARDWARE DESCRIPTION LANGUAGE

by

Donald E. Thomas
Carnegie Mellon University

and

Philip R. Moorby
Cadence Design Systems, Inc.

KLUWER ACADEMIC PUBLISHERS
Boston/Dordrecht/London

Distributors for North America:
Kluwer Academic Publishers
101 Philip Drive
Assinippi Park
Norwell, Massachusetts 02061 USA

Distributors for all other countries:
Kluwer Academic Publishers Group
Distribution Centre
Post Office Box 322
3300 AH Dordrecht, THE NETHERLANDS

Consulting Editor: Jonathan Allen, Massachusetts Institute of Technology

Library of Congress Cataloging-in-Publication Data
Thomas, D.E. (Donald E.), 1951-
    The Verilog hardware description language / by Donald E. Thomas and Phillip R. Moorby.
        p. cm.
    Includes index.
    ISBN 0-7923-9126-8 (alk. paper)
    1. Verilog (Computer hardware description language) I. Moorby,
Phillip R., 1953-   . II. Title.
TK7885.7.T48 1991
621.39'2--dc20   90-48370
                                                                          CIP

To Sandie and Teresa,
and John and Holland,
and Jill.

Table of Contents

Preface

The Verilog language is a hardware description language which provides a means of specifying a digital system at a wide range of levels of abstraction. The language supports the early conceptual stages of design with its behavioral level of abstraction, and the later implementation stages with its structural level of abstraction. The language provides hierarchical constructs, allowing the designer to control the complexity of a description.

Verilog was originally designed in the winter of 1983/84 as a proprietary verification/simulation product. Since then, several other proprietary analysis tools have been developed around the language, including a fault simulator and a timing analyzer; the language being instrumental in providing consistency across these tools. Now, the language is openly available for any tool to read and write. This book introduces the language.

It is sometimes difficult to separate the language from the simulator tool because the dynamic aspects of the language are defined by the way the simulator works. Where possible, we have stayed away from simulator-specific details and concentrated on design specification, but have included enough information to be able to have working executable models.

The book takes a tutorial approach to presenting the language. Indeed, we start with a tutorial introduction which presents, via examples, the major features of the language. We then continue with a more complete discussion of the language constructs. Numerous examples are provided to allow the reader to easily learn (and relearn!) by example. Finally, in the appendix we provide a formal description of the language. Overall, our approach is to provide a means of learning by observing the examples, and doing the exercises.

We have provided a set of exercises to stimulate thought while reading the book. It is strongly recommended that you try the exercises as early as possible with the aid of the Verilog simulator. Or, if you have your own designs, or some from a data book, try them out too. The examples shown in the book are available in electronic form from Cadence Design Systems, Inc. by sending a request to receive the examples to the e-mail address "thomasmoorbybook@cadence.com".

The book assumes a knowledge of introductory logic design and software programming. As such, the book is of use to practicing integrated circuit design engineers, and undergraduate and graduate electrical or computer engineering students. The tutorial introduction provides enough information for students in an introductory logic design course to make simple use of logic simulation as part of their laboratory experience. The rest of the book could then be used in upper level logic design and architecture courses.

The book is organized into seven chapters and six appendicies. We start with the tutorial introduction to the language in chapter 1. Chapters 2 and 3 present the language's behavioral modeling constructs. Chapters 4 and 5 then present logic level modeling, and chapter 6 presents the more advanced topic of switch level modeling. Finally, chapter 7 shows sizable examples of the use of the language. The appendicies are reserved for the dryer topics typically found in a language manual. Read them at your own risk.

D. E. Thomas
P. R. Moorby

Acknowledgements

The authors would like to acknowledge the many people in Cadence Design Systems, Inc. and the customers of the Verilog-based products who have contributed to the continuing development of the Verilog language. In particular, the authors would like to thank Leigh Brady for her help in reviewing the manuscript.

1. Verilog -- A Tutorial Introduction

1.1 DESCRIBING DIGITAL SYSTEMS

Digital systems are highly complex. At their most detailed level, they may consist of over a million elements, as would be the case if we viewed a system as a collection of logic gates or pass transistors. From a more abstract viewpoint, these elements may be grouped into a handful of functional components such as cache memories, floating point units, signal processors, or real-time controllers. Hardware description languages have evolved to aid in the design of systems with this large number of elements and wide range of electronic and logical abstractions.

The creative process of digital system design begins with a conceptual idea of a logical system to be built, a set of constraints that the final implementation must meet, and a set of primitive components from which to build the system. Design is an iterative process of either manually proposing or automatically synthesizing alternative solutions and then testing them with respect to the given constraints. The design is typically divided into many smaller subparts (following the well-known divide-and-conquer engineering approach) and each subpart is further divided, until the whole design is specified in terms of known primitive components.

The Verilog language provides the digital system designer with a means of describing a digital system at a wide range of levels of abstraction, and, at the same time, provides access to computer-aided design tools to aid in the design process at these levels. The language supports the early conceptual stages of design with its behavioral constructs, and the later implementation stages with its structural constructs. During the design process, behavioral and structural constructs may be mixed as the logical structure of portions of the design are designed. The description may be simulated to determine correctness, and some synthesis tools exist for automatic design. Indeed, the Verilog language provides the designer entry into the world of large, complex digital systems design. This first chapter provides a brief tour of the basic features of the Verilog language.

1.2 GETTING STARTED

The Verilog language describes a digital system as a set of *modules*. Each of these modules has an interface to other modules as well as a description of its contents. A module represents a logical unit that can be described either by specifying its internal logical structure -- for instance describing the actual logic gates it is comprised of, or by describing its behavior in a program-like manner -- in this case focusing on what the module does rather than on its logical implementation. These modules are then interconnected with nets, allowing them to communicate.

1.2.1 A Structural Description

We start with one of the basic logic circuits from introductory logic design courses: the NAND latch shown in Example 1.1. The latch has two outputs which, when legal inputs are provided, are complementary. When both inputs are one, the latch holds its value. However, when one of the inputs becomes a zero, the output of the NAND gate it is attached to is forced to a one, the other NAND gate's output is forced to a zero, which feeds back to the first NAND and holds its output at a one. The same is true for the other input. Zeros on both inputs is an illegal condition.

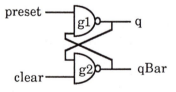

```
module ffNand;
    wire    q, qBar;
    reg     preset, clear;

    nand #1
        g1 (q, qBar, preset),
        g2 (qBar, q, clear);
endmodule
```

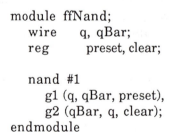

Example 1.1. A Simple NAND Latch.

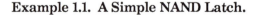

A Verilog description of this circuit is also shown in Example 1.1. The description shows the basic *definition* of a module -- in this case, of a module named **ffNand**. Each module definition includes the keyword module and its name and is terminated by the *endmodule* statement. The second line of this definition specifies the names of *wires* used to transmit logic values among the submodules of this module. The third line declares the names of storage elements that will hold values. These *registers* are an abstraction of a flip flop circuit element.

The fifth line, and its continuation onto lines 6 and 7, *instantiates* two NAND gates each having a delay of one time unit. NAND gates are one of the predefined logic gate types in the language -- the others, including AND, OR, and XOR, will be detailed at a later time. This statement specifies that two gates, called **g1** and **g2**, exist in the circuit, and that they are connected to the wires and registers shown. The first label in the parentheses is the gate's output and the others are inputs. The wire, register, and instance names are included in the schematic drawing to further clarify the correspondence between the logic diagram and its equivalent Verilog description.

Although this example is simple, it illustrates several important points about the Verilog language. The first is the notion of module *definition* versus module *instantiation*. Using the module statement, as shown in the above example, we define a module once specifying all of its inner detail. This module may then be used (instantiated) in the design many times. Each of these instantiations are called instances of the module, and can be separately named and connected differently. Gates, like the NAND, are predefined logic primitives provided by the language. They are presented in more detail in Chapter 4.

The gates are connected by *nets*. Nets are one of the two fundamental data types of the language (registers are the other), and are used to model an electrical connection between structural entities such as gates. A *wire* is one type of net; others include *wired-AND*, *wired-OR,* and *trireg* connections. Except for the *trireg* net which models a wire as a capacitor that stores electrical charge, nets do not store values. Rather, they only transmit values that are driven on them. The different net types are described in more detail in Chapters 4 and 6.

We have also seen how several gates are built into larger modules in a *hierarchical* manner. In this example, NAND gates were used to build the **ffNand** module. This **ffNand** module could then be used as a piece of a larger module by instantiating it into another module, and so on. The use of hierarchical descriptions allows us to control the complexity of a design by breaking the design into smaller and more meaningful chunks (i.e. submodules). When instantiating the submodules, all we need know about them is their interface; their potentially complex implementation details are described elsewhere and thus do not clutter the current module's description.

As a final comment, we should point out that the designation of the **preset** and **clear** as registers seems rather anomalous. One would think that **q** would be the register, **qBar** its complemented output, and **preset** and **clear** just wires driving the circuit. In this description, **q** and **qBar** are the wires driven by the outputs of the instantiated NAND gates and **preset** and **clear** are inputs to these gates. As we will see in the more-complete form of this example in the next section, **preset** and **clear** are defined as registers to aid in simulation.

1.2.2 Simulating the NAND Latch

Example 1.2 shows a more complete module definition for **ffNand**. The example includes statements that will provide stimulus to the NAND gate instances, and statements that will monitor the changes in their outputs.

A simulator for a digital system is a program that executes the statements in the above *initial* statement (and as we will see later, the *always* statement), and propagates changed values from the outputs of gates and registers to other gate and module inputs. A simulator is further characterized by its ability to keep track of *time*, causing the changed values to appear at some specified time in the future rather than immediately. These future changes are typically stored in a time-ordered event queue. When the simulator has no further statement execution or value propagation to perform at the current time, it finds the next time-ordered event from the event queue, updates time to that of the event, and executes the event. This event may or may not generate events at future times. This simulation loop continues until there are no more events to be simulated or the user halts the simulation by some other means.

```verilog
module ffNand;
    wire    q, qBar;
    reg     preset, clear;

    nand #1
        g1 (q, qBar, preset),
        g2 (qBar, q, clear);

    initial
        begin
        // two slashes introduce a single line comment
        $monitor ($time,,
            "Preset = %b clear = %b q = %b qBar = %b",
            preset, clear, q, qBar);
        //waveform for simulating the nand flip flop
        #10 preset = 0; clear = 1;
        #10 preset = 1;
        #10 clear = 0;
        #10 clear = 1;
        #10 $finish;
        end
endmodule
```

Example 1.2. NAND Latch To Be Simulated.

Example 1.2 differs from Example 1.1 with the inclusion of the *initial* statement. The simulator begins the simulation by starting the execution of the initial statement. The results of the simulation of this example are shown in Example 1.3.

The first statement in the initial is a simulation command to monitor (and print) a set of values when any one of the values changes. In this case, the quoted string is printed with the values of **preset, clear, q**, and **qBar** substituted for the %b (for binary) printing control in the string. When issued, the monitor command prints the initial values. As shown in Example 1.3, they print as **x** meaning unknown.

The initial statement continues by scheduling four events to occur in the future. The statement:

```verilog
#10     preset = 0;  clear = 1;
```

specifies that registers **preset** and **clear** will be loaded with zero and one respectively 10 time units from the current time. The simulator suspends the execution of this initial statement by putting these two value changes into the event queue for propagation at time 10. At that time, the initial statement will be reactivated.

The simulator sees no other action at the current (zero) time and goes to the next event in the time-ordered event queue. At this time (time 10), the changed values (**preset** and **clear**) are propagated. By propagation, we mean that every primitive gate that is connected to either **preset** or **clear** is notified of the change. These gates may then schedule their outputs to change in the future. Because the gates in this example are defined to have a time delay of 1, their output changes will be propagated one time unit into the future (at time 11).

```
 0 preset=x clear=x q=x qBar=x
10 preset=0 clear=1 q=x qBar=x
11 preset=0 clear=1 q=1 qBar=x
12 preset=0 clear=1 q=1 qBar=0
20 preset=1 clear=1 q=1 qBar=0
30 preset=1 clear=0 q=1 qBar=0
31 preset=1 clear=0 q=1 qBar=1
32 preset=1 clear=0 q=0 qBar=1
40 preset=1 clear=1 q=0 qBar=1
```

Example 1.3. Results of Simulating Example 1.2.

Since we are still at time 10 in the simulation, the initial statement continues with the next line which specifies that in 10 *more* time units (i.e. at time 20), **preset** will be loaded with a one. This value is put into the event queue for propagation at time 20, and the next event is taken from the queue. This event, at time 11, is the result of **preset** being zero -- i.e. **q** becomes 1. The value of **q** is propagated to the input of NAND gate **g2** which is then scheduled to propagate its changed output one time unit in the future (time 12).

The simulation continues until there are no further changes in the initial statement nor in the logic gates. Specifically, at time 20, **preset** is set to 1 and the q and **qBar** outputs remain constant. At time 30, **clear** is set to zero and the flip flop changes state after two gate delays. **Clear** is set to 1 at time 40 and the outputs remain constant. At time 50, the **finish** command stops the simulation and returns control to the host operating system.

The simulator output in Example 1.3 illustrates three of the four values that a bit may have in the simulator: 1 (TRUE), 0 (FALSE), and x (unknown). The fourth value, z, is used to model the high impedance states of tristate gates.

We now can see why **preset** and **clear** were defined as registers for the examples of this section. As the only "external" inputs to the two NAND gates (**q** and **qBar** are outputs of the NAND gates), we needed a means of setting and holding their value during the simulation. Since wires do not hold values -- they merely transmit values from outputs to inputs -- the register mechanism was used to hold the **preset** and **clear** inputs.

As a final comment on the simulation of this example, we should note that simulation times have been described in terms of "time units". A Verilog description is written with time delays specified as we have shown above. The *timescale* compiler directive is then used to attach units and a precision (for rounding) to these numbers. The examples in the book will not specify the actual time units.

1.3 MODULE HIERARCHY

Let's begin building a larger example that includes more and varied components. Figure 1.1 illustrates pictorially what our design looks like. In this section we will detail each of the modules and their interconnection.

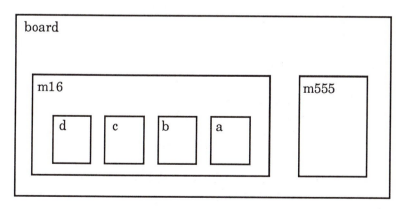

Figure 1.1. The Counter Example.

The example consists of a **board** module which contains a clock module (**m555**) and a four-bit counter (**m16**). The counter is further broken down into four D-type flip flops (labeled **a** through **d**).

1.3.1 The Counter

We look first at the counter module definition as shown in Example 1.4. Our previous **ffNand** example had neither inputs nor outputs -- a rather limiting situation that does not help in developing a module hierarchy -- and this example extends our notion of defining modules to include ones that have ports.

The first line is the opening module definition statement where the module *ports* are shown in parentheses. Within the module, these ports must be declared to be *inputs, outputs,* or bidirectional *inouts.* The example declares that output port **value** is a 4-bit *vector.* The square brackets ("[ ]") construct declares the range of bit numbers that the output has, the first number being the most significant bit and the second being the least significant bit. The bit numbers used in the specifications must be positive. **Fifteen** and **altFifteen** are then declared as single bit (or *scaler*) outputs, and **clock** is declared as a single bit input.

We have introduced the terms *vector* and *scaler* in describing this example. Registers and nets which are single-bit are said to be scaler. Registers and nets, which are declared to have a range of bits as indicated by the square brackets ("[ ]") construct, are vectors.

```
module m16 (value, clock, fifteen, altFifteen);
    output  [3:0]   value;
    output          fifteen,
                    altFifteen;
    input           clock;

    dEdgeFF   a (value[0], clock, ~value[0]),
              b (value[1], clock, value[1] ^ value[0]),
              c (value[2], clock, value[2] ^ &value[1:0]),
              d (value[3], clock, value[3] ^ &value[2:0]);

    assign fifteen = value[0] & value[1] & value[2] & value[3];
    assign altFifteen = &value;
endmodule
```

Example 1.4. A 16-Bit Counter.

Next, instances of a module named **dEdgeFF** are instantiated to model the four bits of the counter. Since the order of the names in the instantiation port list must match the order of ports in the definition, we need to know the order of port names (this is analogous to the software situation where we need to know the order of parameters when calling a subroutine). The **dEdgeFF** module, which will be defined in the next section, has the following module name and port definition order:

dEdgeFF (q, clock, data).

The D-type flip flops are instantiated, and their single bit outputs are connected to the individual bits of the output **value**. Thus, D-type flip flop **a** has its output connected to bit 0 of **value** (the least significant bit), the **clock** input to module **m16** is connected to the **clock** input of the D-type flip flop, and the complement ("~") of the 0th bit of **value** is connected to the flip flop's **data** input. The rest of the circuit is connected as a synchronous counter, each flip flop being clocked by the single **clock** input. The **data** input to instance **b** of the **dEdgeFF** is the exclusive-OR ("^") of bits zero and one of **value**. The **data** inputs to instances **c** and **d** will be described shortly.

This example also introduces the use of the *assign* statement which is another way of describing a combinational logic function. The two assign statements show two means of generating a logic one output when each of the flip flops hold a one (i.e. taken together the four flip flops hold the value 15 decimal). The first shows the output **fifteen** being assigned the logical AND of the individual bits of **value** using the **&** operator. This operator may be used to AND scaler or vector operands together. The second method shows **&** being used as a unary *reduction* operator; all of the bits of the vector operand on the right-hand side are ANDed together. Thus the two logical values are the same, just specified differently.

We now can explain the **data** inputs to instances **c** and **d** of the **dEdgeFF**. Instance **c**'s **data** input is the exclusive-OR of bit 2 of **value** with the reduction-AND of bits one and zero of **value**. That is, "&value[1:0]" specifies that the two bits of **value** are ANDed together. This result is then exclusive-ORed with bit 2 of **value**. The construct "value[1:0]" is called a *part select* of a vector -- only a selected range of bits from the entire vector is used in the operation.

The *assign* statements are called *continuous assignment* statements. Essentially we described an AND gate with four inputs and an output connected (assigned) to **m16**'s output **fifteen**. The assign statement allows us to describe a combinational logic function without regard to its actual structural implementation -- that is, there are no instantiated modules with port connections. In a simulation of the circuit, the result of the logical expression on the right-hand side of the equal sign is evaluated anytime one of its inputs changes and the result drives the output **fifteen**. The assign statement is discussed further in Chapter 4.

1.3.2   Components of the Counter

The **m16** counter is composed of four negative edge triggered D-type flip flops which are defined in Example 1.5.

```
module dEdgeFF (q, clock, data);
    output  q ;
    reg     q ;
    input   clock, data;

    initial
      q = 0;

    always
      @(negedge clock) #10 q = data;

endmodule
```

Example 1.5. A D-Type Edge-Triggered Flip Flop.

The edge-triggered flip flop is defined to have two inputs and one output. In addition, there is a register named **q** that (implicitly) drives output **q**. In this example, register **q** directly models the flip flop's storage bit. When this module is simulated, its state is initialized to be zero as specified in the initial statement.

This example introduces the behavioral approach to modeling hardware. The functionality of the module is described in terms of procedural statements rather than with module instantiations. The *always* statement, introduced here, is the basis for modeling sequential behavior. The always statement, essentially a "while (TRUE)" statement, includes one or more *procedural* statements that are repeatedly executed. These procedural statements execute much like you would expect a software program to execute: changing register values, and executing loops and conditional expressions.

This always statement contains only one statement:

@(negedge clock) #10 q = data;

The statement specifies that when there is a negative edge on the **clock** input, then after 10 time units, register **q** will be loaded with the value on the **data** input.

Thus we have behaviorally modeled a negative edge triggered flip flop by using Verilog's procedural statements. The behavioral description captures all of the functionality of the module but leaves the actual logical implementation open to the designer.

Behavioral modeling is not limited to describing actions on clock edges. Rather, Verilog provides language semantics that are similar to those found in high-level software programming languages such as the C language. Thus statements to describe loops, conditionals, and subroutines are available. These are described in Chapters 2 and 3.

1.3.3   A Clock for the System

Our counter needs a clock to drive it. Example 1.6 defines an abstraction of a "555" timer chip called **m555**.

```
module m555 (clock);
    output  clock;
    reg     clock;

    initial
        #5 clock = 1;

    always
        #50 clock = ~ clock;
endmodule
```

Example 1.6. A Clock For the Counter.

The **m555** module has an internal register (**clock**) which is also the output of the module. The clock is initialized to be one after 5 time units have passed. The **m555** is further modeled behaviorally with an always statement which states that after 50 time units **clock** will be loaded with its complement. Since an always statement is essentially a "while (TRUE)" loop, after the first 50 time units have passed, the always statement will be scheduled to execute and change its value in another 50 time units; i.e. this time at time 100 time units. Because **clock** will change value every 50 time units, we have created a clock with a period of 100 time units.

We may want to specify the clock period with real time units. The *timescale* compiler directive is used to specify the time units of any delay operator (#), and the precision to which time calculations will be rounded. If the compiler directive

'timescale 1ns / 100ps

was placed before a module definition, then all delay operators in that module and any module that followed it would be in units of nanoseconds and any time calculations would be internally rounded to the nearest one hundred picoseconds.

1.3.4   Tying the Whole Circuit Together

We have now defined the basic modules to be used in our system. What remains is the tying of these together to complete the design shown in Figure 1.1. Example 1.7 ties together the module definitions in Examples 1.4, 1.5, and 1.6 by defining another module (called **board**) that instantiates and interconnects these modules. This is shown graphically in Figure 1.2

```
module board();
    wire    [3:0] count;
    wire          clock,
                  f,
                  af;

    m16     counter (count, clock, f, af);
    m555    clockGen (clock);

    always @ (posedge clock)
        $display ($time,,,"count=%d, f=%d, af=%d", count, f, af);
endmodule
```

Example 1.7. The Top-Level Module of the Counter.

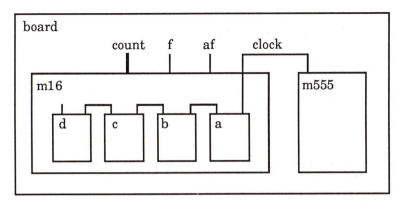

Figure 1.2. The Counter Example With Some Connections Shown.

Most of the statements in the board module definition have previously been described, however the $display statement in the always statement is new. This statement is similar to a print statement in a programming language. The current simulation time will be printed followed by the quoted string with the values of the listed variables substituted in for the printing controls (printing controls are indicated by a percent sign followed by a letter). The %d printing control indicates that the value will be printed as an unsigned decimal integer. The ",,," put extra spaces between the display of the time and the quoted string. In combination with the always statement, the printout will display these values at the positive edge of the clock.

A few words of further explanation are in order. The two modules (**counter** and **clockGen**) are interconnected with the **clock** wire. This wire is driven by the output of module **clockGen**, an instance of the **m555** timer, and is input to module **counter**, an instance of the counter. Although the name **clock** was also used in the module definitions of **m16** and **m555**, we could have chosen another name for the wire that connects them. Essentially, names of entities such as wires and registers are known only in the module where they are declared. Thus the **clock** in module **m555** is different from the **clock** in **m16** and are only connected together because module **board** connects them with a wire that also happens to be named **clock**.

If the module definitions in Examples 1.4, 1.5, 1.6, and 1.7 are compiled together, they form a complete description and can be simulated.

1.4   BEHAVIORAL MODELING

Our view so far of the Verilog language has mainly highlighted its capabilities of describing structure -- module definitions, module instances, and their interconnections. We have only had a very cursory view of the language's capability for describing a module's function behaviorally.

A *behavioral* model of a module is an abstraction of how the module works. The outputs of the module are described in terms of its inputs, but no effort is made to describe how the module is implemented in terms of logic gates.

Behavioral models are useful early in the design process. At that point, a designer is more concerned with simulating the system's intended behavior to understand its gross performance characteristics with little regard to its final implementation. Later, structural models with accurate detail of the final implementation are substituted and resimulated to demonstrate functional correctness. In terms of the design process, the key point is that it is often useful to describe and simulate a module using a behavioral description before deciding on the module's actual structural implementation. This behavioral model can then be the starting point for synthesizing several alternate structural implementations of the behavior.

The behavioral models are described with a language similar to a programming language. As we will see, there are many levels of abstraction at which we may model the behavior of a system. For large systems, we may describe the algorithm that it is to implement. Indeed, the algorithm may be an almost direct translation from a programming language such as C. At a lower level of abstraction, we may describe the register-transfer level behavior of a circuit, specifying the clock edges and preconditions for each of the system's register transfers. At a still lower level, we may describe the behavior of a logic gate or flip flop. In each case, we use the behavioral modeling constructs of the Verilog language to specify the function of a module without directly specifying its implementation.

1.4.1   A Behavioral Model of the m16 Counter

In a structural description such as **m16** in Example 1.4, we described how the module consisted of other modules and their interconnections. A behavioral model of the **m16** would not have concerned itself with the submodules. Rather it would only have described how the counter value incremented on the negative edge of the clock. Example 1.8 shows an alternate behavioral definition of m16, **m16Behav.**

```
module m16Behav (value, clock, fifteen, altFifteen);
    output   [3:0]  value;
    reg      [3:0]  value;
    output          fifteen,
                    altFifteen;
    reg             fifteen,
                    altFifteen;
    input           clock;

    initial
        value = 0;

    always
        begin
        @(negedge clock)  #10 value = value + 1;
        if (value == 15)
            begin
                altFifteen = 1;
                fifteen = 1;
            end
        else
            begin
                altFifteen = 0;
                fifteen = 0;
            end
        end
endmodule
```

Example 1.8.
The Counter Module Described With Behavioral Statements.

This description shows the counter having the same ports as the structural version. However, the rest of the description of the module is specified quite differently. **value, fifteen,** and **altFifteen** are declared to be registers. The declaration of the registers and outputs of the same name implicitly connect the outputs of the registers to the ports. As before, the always statement provides the means of describing the behavior. Essentially it triggers on the negative edge of **clock** and then increments **value** after 10 time units. If **value** is then equal to 15, the outputs **altFifteen** and **fifteen** are set to 1. Otherwise they are set to zero. The always statement then triggers on the next negative edge on **clock**.

Arithmetic operations are performed modulo 2^n, where n is the bit width of the operation. Thus, when the 4-bit register **value** is equal to 15, then after being incremented again, it will be zero.

In contrast to the previous structural description of **m16**, the actual implementation of **m16Behav** is not specified. Rather the module is specified behaviorally and the description serves as a starting point for alternate implementations. Further, **value, fifteen,** and **altFifteen** are declared to be registers. In behavioral descriptions, we use procedural statements to describe the module's functionality and these require the use of registers (or variables in software programming) to store the values. The structural version of **m16** did not use registers, rather it implicitly connected the output drivers in the instantiated flip flops to the output port with a wire.

The behavioral description in Example 1.8 is correct, but not as exact as it could be. Although the sizes of the registers and ports are all specified, the sizes of the constants used in the description are not. As it turns out, the description is correct because the right-most n bits of the right-hand side of a statement are stored in the n-bit operand on the left-hand side of the equal sign. As we will see later, there are times when exact bit width specifications are necessary. The statement

   altFifteen = 0;

could be written more exactly as

   altFifteen = 1'b0;

meaning that the one-bit operand with value zero specified in binary is loaded into register **altFifteen**. The issue of whether to use one specification versus another is a matter of readability and exactness. Appendix A shows how numbers may be specified with other number bases.

We could now simulate our **board** module with either of the two **m16** modules and obtain the same results.

1.4.2   Mixing Structure and Behavior

The natural evolution of a digital system design is from abstract behavior to detailed, implementable structure. Along this design path, the design will be represented at times by a mixture of behavioral and structural modules. These two types of models may exist for two reasons. First, not all modules of a design will be designed down to the detailed structural level at the same time -- certain, more critical, parts will be worked on first. Secondly, part of a design may make use of off-the-shelf (pre-designed) hardware. In both cases, parts of the description will be behavioral and parts will be structural.

We now consider the details of intermixing both behavioral and structural models by examining the description of the Fibonacci number generator shown in Figure 1.3 In this system we will have a number generator module (**ng**) that produces a number n and passes it onto the Fibonacci number generator module (**fng**) that will calculate the nth Fibonacci number. A latch (**ready**) is provided for the two modules to signal when to pass another number.

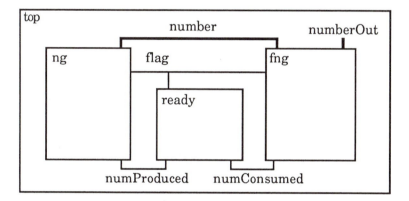

Figure 1.3. The Fibonacci Number Generator.

The behavioral descriptions in **ng** and **fng** execute concurrently and pass information when the latch output indicates that previous data has been consumed and new valid data is ready. Thus, the latch acts as a data-valid signal for a single element queue between producer and consumer modules. Module **top** in Example 1.9 shows the interconnections between the modules. The output of the **nandLatch** (**flag**) is provided to the other modules, the **fibNumberGen** module (**fng**) is able to set the latch by sending a pulse on the **numConsumed** wire, and the **numberGen** module (**ng**) is able to reset it by sending a pulse on the **numProduced** wire. The 16-bit wire **number** carries the value whose Fibonacci number is to be calculated between the modules. Even though there are four ports defined for the **nandLatch**, Example 1.9 shows the second one (**qBar**) being left unconnected.

```
module top();
    wire            flag, numProduced, numConsumed;
    wire [15:0]     number, numberOut;

    nandLatch       ready (flag, , numConsumed, numProduced);
    numberGen       ng (number, numProduced, flag);
    fibNumberGen    fng (number, flag, numConsumed,
                                        numberOut);
endmodule
```

Example 1.9. Top Level of the Fibonacci Number Generator.

The latch is a simple NAND latch similar to that of Example 1.1. However, for this example we include ports on the latch as shown in Example 1.10.

```
module nandLatch (q, qBar, set, reset);
    output  q, qBar;
    input   set, reset;

    nand #2
        (q, qBar, set),
        (qBar, q, reset);
endmodule
```

Example 1.10. A NAND Latch.

Other differences from the previous latch example include a different delay time (2 instead of 1 time unit) and the fact that the NAND instances are not individually named. Instances of primitive gates, such as NAND and NOR, need not be individually named. However, instances of modules must be named as shown above in Example 1.9.

The **numberGen** module is defined behaviorally in Example 1.11. The first statement of the always statement shows it *wait*ing for input **flag** to be one. As soon as conditions in other parts of the design make the wait condition TRUE, the always statement can then continue executing. In this example, **flag** is the **q** output of the **nandLatch** which, when set, signifies that the previous value has been received and another can be generated. When module **fibNumberGen** sets the latch, **flag** will become one, a delay of 100 time units will occur and then another seed-**number** will be generated. **numProduced** is then set to zero for 10 time units. Since output **numProduced** is connected to the **nandLatch**'s **reset** port, the latch will clear signifying that a new number is available.

```
module numberGen (number, numProduced, flag);
    output  [15:0]  number;
    output          numProduced;
    input           flag;

    reg             numProduced;
    reg     [15:0]  number;

    initial
      begin
        number = 3;
        numProduced = 1;
      end

    always
      begin
        wait (flag == 1)
          #100 number = number + 1;
        numProduced = 0;
        #10 numProduced = 1;
      end
endmodule
```

Example 1.11. The Seed-Number Generator.

On the other side of the latch is module **fibNumberGen**, the Fibonacci number calculator (Example 1.12). The behavior of this module shows that it waits for **flag** to be zero before proceeding with its calculations. Tracing back through the input port, we can see that **flag** is the **q** output of **nandLatch**. Thus, **fibNumberGen** waits on a signal complementary to what **numberGen** waits for. When **flag** becomes zero, the **startingValue** input is copied into **myValue** and a 10 nanosecond pulse is sent out on the **numConsumed** line to set the **nandLatch** and signal module **numberGen** to begin producing another new number.

```
module fibNumberGen (startingValue, flag, numConsumed,
                                          fibNum);
    input   [15:0] startingValue;
    input          flag;
    output         numConsumed;
    output  [15:0] fibNum;

    reg            numConsumed;
    reg     [15:0] myValue;
    reg     [15:0] fibNum;

    initial
       begin
         numConsumed = 0;
         #10 numConsumed = 1;
         $monitor ($time,,
           "fibNum=%d, startingValue=%d",
                 fibNum, startingValue);
       end

    always
       begin
         wait (flag == 0)
           myValue = startingValue;
         numConsumed = 0;
         #10 numConsumed = 1;          //signal ready for input

         for (fibNum = 0; myValue != 0; myValue = myValue - 1)
           fibNum = fibNum + myValue;
         $display ("%d, fibNum=%d", $time, fibNum);
       end
endmodule
```

Example 1.12. The Fibonacci Number Generator Module.

The nth Fibonacci number is calculated in register **fibNum** by the
for loop statement. Within the parentheses of the for statement, the first
statement is the initializing statement for the loop which is executed
once before the loop starts. The second statement is the test for the end of
the loop and is executed before any of the statements in the body of the
loop. The third statement is the loop update statement and is executed
after the statements in the loop body. After the for's parentheses is the
body of the loop. In this example, **fibNum** is initialized to zero, and
while **myValue** (which is a copy of the input value from the **numberGen**
module) is not equal to zero, **myValue** is added to **fibNum** and then

myValue is decremented. When **myValue** becomes zero, the loop ends and **fibNum** and time are displayed. The module then waits for another starting value to be ready.

Notice that module **fibNumberGen** needs a copy of **startingValue** because **startingValue** is an input and we cannot change the value of an input with a procedural statement. (**startingValue** is connected to wire **number** which is driven by the **number** register in module **numberGen**.) Making this copy also allows for concurrency in the design; while **fibNumberGen** works on its copy of **startingValue** in **myValue**, **numberGen** can use register **number** to generate another number.

It is also useful to contrast the wait statement seen in these examples and the event control (@) statement seen in Example 1.8. The event control statement models an edge- triggering mechanism. Control does not pass beyond that point until a value changes (as when Example 1.8 triggered on the negative edge of the clock signal). The wait statement is level sensitive. That is, if the statement is first executed and the expression is TRUE, then the statement will not wait, but continue executing.

1.4.3   Assignment Statements

We have now seen the two different types of assignment statements available in the language. In the structural descriptions (see Example 1.4), we used the *continuous assignment* statement to assign (or connect) the output of an expression to a wire. In the statements:

```
wire a;
assign    a = b | (c & d);
```

where **b**, **c** and **d** could be inputs to the module or registers in the module, the right-hand side of the equal can be thought of as a logic gate whose output is connected to wire **a**. Thus, for any change at any time to **b**, **c**, or **d**, the output of the expression will be evaluated and made to drive wire **a**.

An equivalent way of writing these two statements is through a wire definition

```
wire      a = b | (c & d);
```

Note that in both cases we have used parentheses to signify that the AND (&) operation is done before the OR (|). Actually these are not necessary because the precedence of the & operator is higher than |, and thus the & would be done first anyway. However, we like to specify complex statements with parentheses because most of us do not remember all of the precedence rules. (For those sticklers for detail, the Verilog precedence rules are given in Appendix B.)

Procedural assignment, also using =, can only assign values to registers or memory elements. The assignment (actually a loading of the value into the register or memory) is done only when control is transferred to the procedural assignment statement. Thus, even though the values of the registers and/or wires in the expressions on the right-hand side of the assignment may change at any time, the resulting value is only evaluated and loaded when control is transferred to the statement. In this way, a procedural assignment functions like a normal software programming language assignment statement. Procedural statements are found only in initial and always statements, and in functions and tasks as will be discussed in Chapter 2.

In essence, the two types of assignments are closely aligned with the two fundamental data types of the language: nets and registers. Continuous assigns may only drive nets, and procedural assignments may only be made to registers.

1.4.4 Mixing Behavioral and Structural Descriptions

The examples in this section illustrate how structural and behavioral description can easily be combined. The output of registers and memories in behavioral descriptions can be assigned (with a continuous assignment) to wires as is shown implicitly in module **fibNumberGen**. **numConsumed** is a register that is connected to an output port of the module. In module **top**, that port is connected to wire **numConsumed** that drives input **set** of the **nandLatch**.

Further, wires can be attached explicitly to a register as in the following statements:

```
reg    [15:0]   x ;
wire   [15:0]   y = x;
```

Here, wire **y** is connected to the output of register **x**. Anytime **x** is loaded procedurally with a new value, it will drive wire **y** and the inputs it is connected to with that new value.

Wires may also be used in procedural assignment statements, but only on the right-hand side. Module **fibNumberGen** illustrates this with the statement:

    myValue = startingValue;

in the wait statement. Here **startingValue** is an input to the module coming from the external wire **number** in module **top**. Whatever value is currently being driven on the wire will be used in the procedural expression.

1.5 SUMMARY

This brief tour has illustrated the basic capabilities of the language. Important among these are:

- The ability to break a design into modules which can then be further divided until the design is specified in terms of basic logic primitives. This hierarchical modularization allows a designer to control the complexity of the design through the well-known divide-and-conquer approach to large engineering design.

- The ability to describe a design either in terms of the abstract behavior of the design or in terms of its actual logical structure. The behavioral description allows for early design activities to concentrate on functionality. When the behavior is agreed upon, then it becomes the specification for designing possibly several alternate structural implementations.

The rest of the book illustrates, in more depth, the syntax and semantics of the Verilog language.

1.6 EXERCISES

1.1 Rewrite the NAND latch in Example 1.2 with continuous assignment statements.

1.2 Change the clock generator **m555** in Example 1.6 such that the clock period remains the same but that the low pulse width is 40 and high pulse width is 60.

1.3 Change the entire **if** statement in Example 1.8 to use only two equivalent assignment statements.

1.4 Add an instance of **m16Behav** in Example 1.8 to module **board** in Example 1.7 and parallelize the two forms of the counter. Choose different net names for the outputs of **m16** and **m16Behav** and write a single continuous assignment that compares **value**, **fifteen**, and **altFifteen** outputs for any differences. The left-hand side of the continuous assignment is to be a scalar net which is driven to 1 if there is a difference. Consult Appendix B for information on extra operators that may be needed. Simulate the description and monitor the results, explaining any differences.

1.5 Keeping the same output timing, replace the initial and always statements in the clock generator **m555** in Example 1.6 with gate primitives.

2. Behavioral Modeling Constructs

We now begin a more in-depth discussion of the constructs used to model the behavior of digital systems. These have been split into two groups. The first are statements that are, for the most part, similar to those found in programming languages: if-then-else, loops, etc. In the next chapter we take up the statements that are oriented toward modeling the concurrent nature of digital hardware.

2.1 PROCESS MODEL

The basic essence of a behavioral model is the *process*. A process can be thought of as an independent thread of control, which may be quite simple, involving only one repeated action, or very complex, resembling a software program. It might be implemented as a sequential state machine, as a microcoded controller, or as an asynchronous clearing of a register. Several threads may be combined with other threads of control for implementation as a single state machine or they may remain separate in implementation. The point is that we conceive the behavior of digital systems as a set of these independent, but communicating, processes. Their actual implementation is left to the context of the description (what level of abstraction we are dealing with) and the time and area constraints of the implementation.

The basic Verilog statement for describing a process is the *always* statement:

```
always
    statement
```

The always continuously repeats its statement, never exiting or stopping. A behavioral model may contain one or more always statements. (A module that contains none is purely a specification of hierarchical structure -- instantiated submodules and their interconnections.) In terms of a design process using synthesis tools, all of the functionality of the module should be specified within the always statement.

The *initial* statement is similar to the always statement except that it is executed only once.

```
initial
    statement
```

The initial provide a means of initiating input waveforms and other simulation variables before the actual description begins its simulation. Once the statements in the initial are exhausted, it does not repeat, rather it becomes inactive.

The initial and always statements are the basic constructs for describing concurrency. When using these statements, we should be conceptually thinking of concurrently active processes that will interact with each other. Although it is possible to mix the description of behavior between the always and initial statement, it is more appropriate to maintain the separation described here: behavior of the hardware is described in the always, and initialization for the simulation is specified in the initial.

2.2 IF-THEN-ELSE

Conditional statements are used in a sequential behavior description to alter the flow of control. The *if* statement and its variations are common examples of conditional statements. Example 2.1 is a behavioral model of a divide module that shows several new features, including two versions of the **if** statement, with and without an else clause, and the use of parameter definitions.

```
module divide (ddInput, dvInput, quotient, go, done);
    parameter
        DvLen =    15,
        DdLen =    31,
        QLen =     15,
        HiDdMin = 16;

    input   [DdLen:0]   ddInput;
    input   [DvLen:0]   dvInput;
    output  [QLen:0]    quotient;
    input               go;
    output              done;

    reg  [DdLen:0]   dividend;
    reg              done;
    reg  [QLen:0]    quotient;
    reg              negDivisor,
                     negDividend;
    reg  [DvLen:0]   divisor;

always
    begin
        done = 0;
        wait (go);
        divisor = dvInput;
        dividend = ddInput;
        quotient = 0;
        if (divisor)
            begin
              negDivisor = divisor[DvLen];
              if (negDivisor)
                  divisor = - divisor;
              negDividend = dividend[DdLen];
              if (negDividend)
                  dividend = - dividend;
              repeat (DvLen + 1)
                  begin
                      quotient = quotient << 1;
                      dividend = dividend << 1;
                      dividend[DdLen:HiDdMin] =
                          dividend[DdLen:HiDdMin]   - divisor;
                      if (! dividend [DdLen])
                          quotient = quotient + 1;
                      else
                          dividend[DdLen:HiDdMin] =
```

```
                           dividend[DdLen:HiDdMin]  + divisor;
              end
          if (negDivisor != negDividend)
              quotient = - quotient;
        end
      done = 1;
      wait (~go);
    end
  endmodule
```

Example 2.1. A Divide Module.

The **divide** module determines the output **quotient** from the two inputs, **dvInput** and **ddInput**, using an iterative subtract and shift algorithm. First, four parameters are defined. The *parameter* statement defines a name and gives a constant numeric value to it. The name may then be used in the description; on compilation, the numeric value will be substituted.

The divide starts by zeroing the **done** output, which when TRUE would signify that the **quotient** is valid. Then we wait for the **go** input to be one (or TRUE) signifying that the **dvInput** and **ddInput** inputs are valid. When **go** becomes TRUE, **dvInput** and **ddInput** are copied into **divisor** and **dividend** respectively.

The first example of an **if** tests whether the divisor is zero or not with the statement:

```
      if (divisor)
          begin
          // ... statements
          end
```

This shows the basic form of the **if** statement. The **if** is followed by a parenthesized expression; a zero expression evaluates to FALSE and any value other than zero evaluates to TRUE. Comparison with an unknown (**x**) or high impedance (**z**) may produce a result that is either unknown or high impedance. Such a result is interpreted as FALSE. In this case, we are testing the **divisor**. If it is not zero, then we follow the normal divide algorithm. The begin-end block following the **if** statement allows all of the encompassed statements to be considered as part of the **then** statement of the **if**.

Continuing with the divide algorithm, the absolute value of each of the inputs is determined and their original signs are saved. More specifically, the statements

```
negDivisor = divisor[DvLen];
if (negDivisor)
  divisor = - divisor;
```

first assigns (procedurally) bit **DvLen** (i.e. bit 15) of the **divisor** to **negDivisor**. If this bit is a one, indicating that the value was negative in the two's complement number representation, then the **then** part will be executed and **divisor** will be negated, making it positive. It should be noted that since there is no begin-end block with this **if**, the **then** statement is the first statement (up to the semicolon) following the **if**.

This statement also illustrates a *bit select*. A bit select is used to specify that only one of the bits of a vector are to be used in the operation. A range of bits may also be specified by separating the bit numbers specifying the range with a colon. This is called a *part select*.

After the initialization to determine the final arithmetic sign, the **repeat** statement executes the statements in the begin-end block 16 times. Each time, the **quotient** and **dividend** are shifted left one position, as described by the **<<** operator, and then the **divisor** is subtracted from the top part of the **dividend**. If the result of this subtract is positive, one is added to the **quotient**. However, if the result is negative (the top most bit is a one), the **else** part of the **if** conditional statement is executed, adding the **divisor** back into the top part of the **dividend**.

Following this more closely, if the sign bit is 1, then the result is negative. This nonzero value would be interpreted as TRUE by the if statement. However, the **!** operator complements the result and the **if** expression evaluates to FALSE. Thus, if the **dividend** is negative, the **else** part is executed.

Finally, if the signs of the original operands are different, then the **quotient** is negated. After the **quotient** output is calculated, the **done** bit is set to one signalling another module that the output may be read.

Before continuing on, this example illustrates some other facets of the language that should be discussed.

Vector nets and registers all obey the laws of arithmetic modulo 2^n where n is the number of bits in the vector. In effect, the language treats the numbers as unsigned quantities. If any of these values were printed by a $display or $monitor statement, they would be interpreted and printed as unsigned values. However, that does not stop us from writing descriptions of hardware that use the two's complement number representation -- the laws of arithmetic modulo 2^n still hold. Indeed, the unary minus provided in the language performs the correct operation.

The relational operators typically used in conditional expressions are listed in Appendix B. These include > (greater than), >= (greater than or equal), == (equal), and != (not equal). In the case where unknown or high impedance values are present, these comparisons may evaluate to a quantity which contains unknown or high impedance values. Such values are considered to be FALSE by the simulator. However, case equality operator (===) and inequality operator (!==) can be used to specify that individual unknown or high impedance bits are to take part in the comparison. For these operators to evaluate to TRUE, the value of each bit being compared, including the unknowns and high impedances, must be equal. Thus, if the statement

```
if (4'b110z === 4'b110z)
    then_statement;
```

were executed, the **then** part of the **if** would be taken. However, if the statement

```
if (4'b110z == 4'b110z)
    then_statement
```

were executed, the **then** part of the **if** would not be taken.

Conditional expressions may be more complex than the single expression examples given so far. Logical expressions may be connected with the && (AND), | | (OR), and ! (NOT) logical operators as shown in the following example:

```
if ((a > b) && ((c >= d) | | (e == f)))
    then_statement
```

In this example, the **then** statement will execute only if **a** is greater than **b**, and either (or both) **c** is greater than or equal to **d**, or **e** equals **f**.

2.2.1   Where Does The ELSE Belong?

Example 2.1 also shows the use of an else clause with an if statement. The else clause is optional, and if it exists, it is paired with the nearest, unfinished if statement.

```
if (! dividend [DdLen])
   quotient = quotient + 1;
else
      dividend[DdLen:HiDdMin] =
         dividend[DdLen:HiDdMin]  + divisor;
```

In this case, if the **dividend** is positive after subtracting the **divisor** from it, then the low order bit of the **quotient** is set to one. Otherwise, we add the **divisor** back into the top part of the **dividend**.

As in most procedural languages, care must be taken in specifying the else clause where multiple if statements are involved. Consider the following situation.

```
if (expressionA)
    if (expressionB)
       a = a + b;
    else
       q = r + s;
```

In this example, we have nested **if** statements and a single **else**. In general, the language attaches the **else** to the nearest **if** statement. In the above situation, if **expressionA** and **expressionB** are both TRUE, then **a** is assigned a new value. If **expressionA** is TRUE and **expressionB** is FALSE, then **q** is assigned a new value. That is, the **else** is paired with the second **if**.

Consider an alternate description giving different results.

```
if (expressionA)
    begin
        if (expressionB)
            a = a + b;
    end
else
    q = r + s;
```

In this example, the begin-end block in the first **if** statement causes the **else** to be paired with the first **if** rather than the second. When in doubt about where the **else** will be attached, use begin-end pairs to make it clear.

2.2.2   The Conditional Operator

The conditional operator (**?:**) can be used in place of the if statement when one of two values is to be selected for assignment. For instance, the statement determining the final sign of the **quotient** in Example 2.1 could have been written with the same result as

quotient = (negDivisor != negDividend) ? -quotient: quotient;.

This operator works as follows: first the conditional expression in the parentheses is evaluated. If it is TRUE (or nonzero), then the value of the right-hand side of the statement is found immediately after the question mark. If it is FALSE, the value immediately after the colon is used. The result of this statement is that one of the two values gets assigned to **quotient**. In this case, if it is true that the signs are not equal, then **quotient** is loaded with its negative. Otherwise, **quotient** remains unchanged. As in Example 2.1, we are describing hardware that will use the two's complement number system, and we use the fact that a Verilog's unary minus operation implements a two's complement negate.

The general form of the conditional operator is:

(expression) ? TRUE_result : FALSE_result

If the **expression** is TRUE, then the value of the operator is the **TRUE_result**. Otherwise the value is the **FALSE_result**.

There is a major distinction between if-then-else and the conditional operator. As an operator, the conditional operator may appear in an expression that is either part of a procedural or continuous assignment statement. The if-then-else construct is a statement that may appear only in the body of an initial or always statement, or in a task or function. Thus whereas if-then-else can only be used in behavioral modeling, the conditional operator can be used both in behavioral and gate level structural modeling.

2.3 LOOPS

Iterative sequential behavior is described with looping statements. Four different statements are provided, including the *repeat, for, while,* and *forever* loops.

2.3.1 Four Basic Loop Statements

An excerpt from Example 2.1 illustrated in Example 2.2 shows the use of the repeat loop.

```
repeat (DvLen + 1)
begin
    quotient = quotient << 1;
    dividend = dividend << 1;
    dividend[DdLen:HiDdMin] =
        dividend[DdLen:HiDdMin]  - divisor;
    if (! dividend [DdLen])
        quotient = quotient + 1;
    else     dividend[DdLen:HiDdMin] =
        dividend[DdLen:HiDdMin]  + divisor;
end
```

Example 2.2. An Excerpt from Example 2.1.

In this form of loop, only a loop count is given in parentheses after the keyword repeat. The value of the loop count expression is determined once at the beginning of the execution of the loop. Then the loop is executed the given number of times. The loop count expression is sampled once at the beginning of the loop, and thus it is not possible to exit the loop execution by changing the loop count variable. The *disable* statements described later allow for early loop exits.

The general form of the repeat statement is

```
repeat (expression)
    statement;
```

The loop in Example 2.2 could have been written as a *for* loop as:

```
for (i = 16; i; i = i - 1)
    begin
        ...//shift and subtract statements
    end
```

In this case, a register must be specified to hold the loop counter. The for loop was also previously shown in Example 1.12, and is very similar in function to for loops in the C programming language. Essentially, this for loop initializes i to 16, and while i is not zero, executes the statements and then decrements i.

The general form of the for loop is

```
for (initial Statement; end Of Loop Expression; loop Update)
    statement
```

Specifically, the initial_statement is executed once at the beginning of the loop. The end Of Loop expression is executed before the body of the loop to determine if we are to stay in the loop. The loop Update statement is executed after the body of the loop and before the next check for end Of Loop. The difference between the for and repeat loop statements is that repeat is simply a means of specifying a constant number of iterations. The for loop is far more flexible and gives access to the loop update variable for control of the end-of-loop-condition.

As in the C programming language, the above for statement could have been written using a *while* statement as:

```
i = 16;
while (i)
    begin
        ...//shift and subtract statements
        i = i - 1;
    end
```

The general form of the while is

```
while (expression)
    statement;
```

The expression is evaluated and if it is TRUE, the statement is executed. The while expression is then evaluated again. Thus, we enter and stay in the loop while the expression is TRUE.

The while statement should not be used to wait for a change in a value generated external to its always statement as illustrated in the following example.

```
module x (inputA);              //This will not work!!
    input    inputA;

    always
        begin
            while (inputA)
                ;     // wait for external variable
            // other statements
        end
endmodule
```

Here, the while statement expression is dependent on the value of **inputA** and the while statement is null. The above while statement appears to have the effect of doing nothing until the value of **inputA** is TRUE, at which time the other statements are executed. However, since we are waiting for an external value to change, the correct statement to use is the *wait*. For further discussion, see the section 3.3 on the wait statement.

Finally, the forever loop loops forever. An example of its use is in the abstract description of a microprocessor.

```
module microprocessor;

    always
       begin
          power-on initializations
          forever
             begin
                fetch and execute instructions
             end
       end
endmodule
```

Example 2.3. An Abstract Microprocessor.

Here we see that certain initializations occur only at power-on time. After that, we remain in the forever loop fetching and executing instructions. A forever loop may be exited by using a *disable* statement, as will be discussed in the next section. If the forever loop is exited, then the always statement will start the power-on initializations and begin the forever loop again.

The general form of the forever loop is:

```
forever
   statement;
```

2.3.2   Exiting Loops on Exceptional Conditions

Generally, a loop statement is written to execute to a "normal" exit. That is, the loop counter is exhausted or the while expressions is no longer TRUE. However, any of the loop statements may be exited through use of the *disable* statement. A disable statement disables, or terminates, any named begin-end block; execution then begins with the statement following the block. Begin-end blocks may be named by placing the name of the block after a colon following the begin keyword. An example of the C programming statements break and continue are illustrated in Example 2.4.

```
begin :break
    for (i = 0; i < n; i = i + 1)
        begin : continue
            if (a == 0)
                disable continue;        // proceed with i = i + 1
            ...//other statements
            if (a == b)
                disable break;           // exit for loop
            ...//other statements
        end
end
```

Example 2.4. Break and Continue Loop Exits.

Example 2.4 shows two named blocks, break and continue. Recall that the continue statement in C skips the rest of the loop body and continues the loop with the loop update, and that the break statement breaks out of the loop entirely, regardless of the loop update and end-of-loop condition. The disable statements in the example perform the analogous actions. Specifically, the **disable continue** statement stops execution of the begin-end block named **continue** and passes control to the update of the for loop. The **disable break** statement stops execution of the block that contains the for loop. Execution would then proceed with the next statement.

Other uses of the disable statement are covered in section 3.4.

2.4   MULTI-WAY BRANCHING

Multi-way branching allows the specification of one or more actions to be taken based on specified conditions. Verilog provides two statements to specify these branches: *if-else-if*, and *case*.

2.4.1   If-Else-If

If-else-if simply uses if-then-else statements to specify multiple actions. It is the most general way to write a multi-way decision in that it allows for a variety of different expressions to be checked in the if conditional expressions. Consider the description of a simple computer shown in Example 2.5. The example is reminiscent of the early Mark-1 computer (a few details have been changed) and is used here for its simplicity.

```
module mark1;
    reg [31:0]   m [0:8191];          // 8192 x 32 bit memory
    reg [12:0]   pc;                  // 13 bit program counter
    reg [31:0]   acc;                 // 32 bit accumulator
    reg [15:0]   ir;                  // 16 bit instruction register

    always
      begin
        ir = m [pc];                  //fetch an instruction
        if (ir[15:13] == 3'b000)      //begin decoding
          pc = m [ir [12:0]];         //and executing
        else if (ir[15:13] == 3'b001)
          pc = pc + m [ir [12:0]];
        else if (ir[15:13] == 3'b010)
          acc = -m [ir [12:0]];
        else if (ir[15:13] == 3'b011)
          m [ir [12:0]] = acc;
        else if ((ir[15:13] == 3'b101) || (ir[15:13] == 3'b100))
          acc = acc - m [ir [12:0]];
        else if (ir[15:13] == 3'b110)
          if (acc < 0) pc = pc + 1;
        #1 pc = pc + 1;                        //increment
                                   program
      end                          // counter and time
endmodule
```

Example 2.5. The Mark-1 Processor With If-Else-If.

This example uses the if-else-if statement to specify the instruction decode of the computer. Bits fifteen through thirteen of the instruction register (ir[15:13]) are compared with seven of the eight possible combinations of three bits. The one that matches determines which of the instructions is executed.

2.4.2   Case

The *case* statement can be used for multi-way branches when each of the if conditionals all match against the same basic expression. Below, the Mark-1 description is rewritten using the case statement for instruction decoding.

```
module mark1Case;
    reg [31:0]  m [0:8191];      // 8192 x 32 bit memory
    reg [12:0]  pc;              // 13 bit program counter
    reg [31:0]  acc;             // 32 bit accumulator
    reg [15:0]  ir;              // 16 bit instruction register

    always
        begin
          ir = m [pc];
          case (ir [15:13])
            3'b000 :  pc = m [ir [12:0]];
            3'b001 :  pc = pc + m [ir [12:0]];
            3'b010 :  acc = -m [ir [12:0]];
            3'b011 :  m [ir [12:0]] = acc;
            3'b100,
            3'b101 :  acc = acc - m [ir [12:0]];
            3'b110 :  if (acc < 0) pc = pc + 1;
          endcase
          pc = pc + 1;
        end
endmodule
```

Example 2.6. The Mark-1 With a Case Statement.

The case expressions are evaluated linearly in the order given in the description. In this case, bits fifteen through thirteen of the instruction register (the *controlling expression*) are compared with each of the eight *case expressions*. If any (or several) of the expressions match the controlling expression, the statement(s) following the colon is executed. The bit widths must match exactly.

The general form of the case statement is

```
case (controlling expression)
    case expression : statement;
endcase
```

Optionally, a default may be specified using the *default* keyword in place of a case expression. When present, the default statement will be executed if none of the other case expressions match the controlling expression. The default may be listed anywhere in the case statement.

The example also illustrates how a single action may be specified for several of the case expressions. The commas between case expressions specify that if either of the comparisons are TRUE, then the statement is executed. In the Mark-1 example, if the three bits have either of the values 4 or 5, a value is subtracted from the accumulator.

2.4.3   Comparison of Case and If-Else-If

In the Mark-1 examples above, either case or if-else-if could be used. Stylistically, the case is more compact in this example and makes for easier reading. Further, since all of the expressions were compared with one controlling expression, the case is stylistically more appropriate. However, there are two major differences between these constructs.

- The conditional expressions in the if-else-if construct are more general. Any set of expressions may be used in the if-else-if whereas with the case statement, the case expressions are all evaluated against a common controlling expression.

- The case expressions may include unknown (x) and high impedance (z) bits. The comparison will succeed only when each bit matches exactly with respect to the values 0, 1, x, and z. Thus it is very important to make sure the expression widths match in the case expressions and controlling expression. In constrast, if statement expressions involving unknown or high impedance values may result in an unknown or high impedance value which will be interpreted as FALSE.

An example of a case statement with unknown and high impedance values is shown below in a debugging example.

```
reg   ready;
// other statements
case (ready)
    1'bz:      $display ("ready is high impedance");
    1'bx:      $display ("ready is unknown");
    default:   $display ("ready is %b", ready);
endcase
```

In this example, the one bit **ready** is compared with high impedance (z) and unknown (x); the appropriate display message is printed during simulation. If **ready** is neither high impedance or unknown, then its value is displayed.

2.4.4   CaseZ and CaseX

Casez and *casex* are two types of case statements that allow don't-care values to be considered in case statements. **Casez** allows for **z** values to be treated as don't-care values, and **casex** allows for both **z** and **x** to be treated as don't-care. In addition to specifying bits as either **z** or **x**, they may also be specified with a question mark ("**?**") which also indicates don't-care. The syntax for **casex** and **casez** is the same as with the case statement, except the **casez** or **casex** keyword is substituted for case.

Consider the following **casex**:

```
module decode;
     reg  [7:0]  r, mask;

     always
       begin
         // other statements
         mask = 8'bx0x0x0x0;
         casex (r ^ mask)
            8'b001100xx:        statement 1;
            8'b1100xx00:        statement 2;
            8'b00xx0011:        statement 3;
            8'bxx001100:        statement 4;
         endcase
       end
endmodule
```

Example 2.7. An Example of Casex.

In this example we have loaded register mask with the eight bit value x0x0x0x0, indicating that every other bit is unknown. If **r** happens to be 8'b01100110, then statement 2 will be executed. Exclusive-ORing these two values together gives the result 8'x1x0x1x0 as can be seen from the following (an unknown exclusive-ORed with anything results in an unknown):

```
     x0x0x0x0
^    01100110
     x1x0x1x0      result of exclusive-or
```

Since the unknown **x** is treated as a don't-care, then only statement 2 will be executed since it is the only case expression where the "do-care" values match up:

```
x1x0x1x0        result of exclusive-or
1100xx00        matching case expression
```

The difference between the two case types is in whether only **z** is considered as a don't-care (**casez**), or whether **z** and **x** are considered don't-cares (**casex**).

2.5 FUNCTIONS AND TASKS

In software programming, functions and procedures are used to break up large programs into more-managable pieces. In Verilog, modules break a design up into more-managable parts, however the use of modules implies that there are structural boundaries being described. These boundaries may in fact model the logical structure or the physical packaging boundaries. Verilog provides *functions* and *tasks* as constructs analogous to software functions and procedures that allow for the behavioral description of a module to be broken into more-managable parts.

As in software programming, functions and tasks are useful for several reasons. They allow often-used behavioral sequences to be written once and called when needed. They also allow for a cleaner writing style; instead of long sequences of behavioral statements, the sequences can be broken into more readable pieces, regardless of whether they are called one or many times. Finally, they allow for data to be hidden from other parts of the design. Indeed, functions and tasks play a key role in making a behavioral description more readable and maintainable.

Consider defining opcode 7 of the Mark-1 description in the previous sections to include a multiply instruction. Early in the behavioral modeling process, we could use the multiply operator as shown in Example 2.8.

```
module mark1Mult;
    //declarations as before

    always
        begin
            ir = m [pc];
            case (ir [15:13])
                3'b000 :  pc = m [ir [12:0]];
                3'b001 :  pc = pc + m [ir [12:0]];
                3'b010 :  acc = -m [ir [12:0]];
                3'b011 :  m [ir [12:0]] = acc;
                3'b100,
                3'b101 :  acc = acc - m [ir [12:0]];
                3'b110 :  if (acc < 0) pc = pc + 1;
                3'b111 :  acc = acc * m [ir [12:0]];     //multiply
            endcase
            #1 pc = pc + 1;
        end
endmodule
```

Example 2.8. The Mark-1 With a Multiply Instruction.

This is a perfectly reasonable behavioral model for early in the design process in that the functionality is thoroughly described. However, we may want to further detail the multiply algorithm used in the design. Our first approach will be to use functions and tasks to describe the multiply algorithm. Later, we will contrast this approach to that of describing the multiply as a separate, concurrently operating module.

2.5.1 Tasks

A Verilog *task* is similar to a software procedure. It is called from a calling statement and after execution, returns to the next statement. It cannot be used in an expression. Parameters may be passed to it and results returned. Local variables may be declared within it and their scope will be the task. Example 2.9 illustrates how module Mark-1 could be rewritten using a task to describe a multiply algorithm.

A task is defined within a module using the *task* and *endtask* keywords. This task is named **multiply** and is defined to have one inout (**a**) and one input (**b**). This task is called from within the always statement. The order of task parameters at the calling site must correspond to the order of definitions within the task. When **multiply** is called, **acc** is copied into task variable **a**, the value read from memory is copied into **b**, and the task proceeds. When the task is ready to return, **prod** is loaded into **a**. On return, **a** is then copied back into **acc** and execution continues after the task call site. Although not illustrated here, a task may include timing and event control statements.

```
module mark1Task;
    //declarations as before

    always
      begin
        ir = m [pc];
        case (ir [15:13])
          // other case expressions as before
          3'b111 :  multiply(acc, m [ir [12:0]]);
        endcase
        pc = pc + 1;
      end

task multiply;
    inout   [31:0]  a ;
    input   [31:0]  b;

    reg   [15:0]   mcnd, mpy;     //multiplicand and multiplier
    reg   [31:0]   prod;          //product

    begin
      mpy  = b[15:0];
      mcnd = a[15:0];
      prod = 0;
      repeat (16)
        begin
          if (mpy[0])
              prod = prod + {mcnd, 16'h0000};
          prod = prod >> 1;
          mpy = mpy >> 1;
        end
      a = prod;
    end
endtask
endmodule
```

Example 2.9. A Task Specification.

The multiply algorithm uses a shift and add technique. The low-order sixteen bits of the operands are multiplied producing a 32-bit result that is returned. The statement

mpy = b[15:0];

does a part select on **b** and loads the low order sixteen bits into **mpy**. Sixteen times, the low-order bit of the multiplier (**mpy**) is checked. If it is one, then the multiplicand (**mcnd**) is concatenated (using the "{ , }" operator) with sixteen bits of zeros on its right and added to the product (**prod**). The product and multiplier are both shifted right one place and the loop continues.

The input, output, and inout parameters declared in tasks (and as we will later see, functions) are local variables separate from the variables named at the calling site. When a task is called, the internal variables declared as inputs or inouts receive copies of the values named at the calling site. The task proceeds executing. When it is done, then all of the variables declared as inouts or outputs are copied back to the variables listed at the call site. When copying values to and from the call site, the variables at the call site are lined up left-to-right with order of the input, output, and inout declarations at the task definition site.

A task may call itself, or be called from tasks that it has called. However, as in a hardware implementation, there is only one set of registers to hold the task variables. Thus, the registers used after the second call to the task are the same physical entities as those in the previous call(s). The simulator maintains the thread of control so that the returns from a task called multiple times are handled correctly.

It is useful to comment on the concatenation operation in the example. The "{ , }" characters are used to express concatenation of values. In this example, we concatenate two 16-bit values together to add to the 32-bit **prod**. **mcnd** has 16 binary zeros (expressed here in hexadecimal format) concatenated onto its right-hand side. Notice that in this case, an exact bit width must be specified for the constant so that **mcnd** is properly aligned with **prod** for the add.

2.5.2 Functions

A Verilog function is similar to a software function. It may be called from within an expression and the one value it returns will be used in the expression. Variables may be declared within the function and their scope will be the function. Unlike a task, a function may not include timing or event control statements. Although not illustrated here, a function may be called from within a continuous assignment. See Section 4.3.

```
module mark1Fun;
    //declarations, as before

    always
       begin
          ir = m [pc];
          case (ir [15:13])
            //case expressions, as before
            3'b111:   acc = multiply(acc, m [ir [12:0]]);
          endcase
          pc = pc + 1;
       end

function [31:0] multiply;
    input   [31:0]  a;
    input   [31:0]  b;

    reg   [15:0]    mcnd,mpy;

    begin
       mpy  = b[15:0];
       mcnd = a[15:0];
       multiply = 0;
       repeat (16)
          begin
            if (mpy[0])
                 multiply = multiply + {mcnd, 16'h0000};
            multiply = multiply >> 1;
            mpy = mpy >> 1;
          end
    end
endfunction
endmodule
```

Example 2.10. A Function Specification.

Example 2.10 shows module **mark1Fun** specified with a multiply function. The function is defined within a module using the *function* and *endfunction* keywords. The function declaration includes the function name and bit width. At calling time, the parameters are copied into the functions inputs; as with tasks, the declaration order is strictly adhered to. The function executes, making assignments to the function's name. On return, the final value of the function's name (multiply) is passed back to the always statement and copied into register **acc**. Every function must have at least one input.

2.5.3 A Structural View

The task and function examples of the previous sections have illustrated different organizations of a behavioral model. That is, we can choose to model the behavior in different ways with the same result. When we used the "*" operator, we were probably only interested in simulation of the model. There are many ways to implement a multiply in hardware, but early in the design process we were content to let the simulator substitute its method.

As the design progresses, we want to specify the multiply algorithm that we want our hardware to implement. This we did by using the task and function statements in the above examples. The implication of the description using a task or function is that this divide algorithm will be part of the final data path and state machine synthesized to implement the Mark-1 processor. That is, we enlarged the behavioral description by specifying the details of the multiply algorithm and thus we would expect the final state machine that implements this behavior to have more states. Likewise, the data path may need more components to hold the values and perform the operations.

Another design decision could have been to use a possibly pre-existing multiply module in conjunction with the Mark-1 module. This case, shown in Example 2.11, illustrates the multiply as an instantiated module within the **mark1Mod** module. This description approach would be used if a previously designed multiply module was to be used, or if the designer wanted to force a functional partitioning of the modules within the design. The **multiply** module ports are connected to the **mark1Mod** and the **mark1Mod** module starts the **multiply** module with the **go** line. When done, the divide module signals the Mark-1 with the **done** line which Mark-1 waits for. This structural description leads to a very different design. Now we have two state machines, one for **mark1Mod** and one for multiply. To keep the two modules synchronized, we have defined a handshaking protocol using wait statements and signalling variables **go** and **done**.

```verilog
module mark1Mod;
    // register declarations as before

    reg  [31:0]   mcnd;
    reg           go;
    wire [31:0]   prod;
    wire          done;
    multiply   mul (prod, acc, mcnd, go, done);

    always
       begin
          go = 0;
          ir = m [pc];
          case (ir [15:13])
            //other case expressions
            3'b111:  begin
                        mcnd = m [ir [12:0]];
                        go = 1;
                        wait (done);
                        acc = prod;
                     end
          endcase
          pc = pc + 1;
       end
endmodule

module multiply (prod, mpy, mcnd, go, done);
    output [31:0] prod;
    input  [31:0] mpy, mcnd;
    input         go;
    output        done;

    reg [31:0]   prod;
    reg [15:0]   myMpy;
    reg          done;

    always
       begin
          done = 0;
          wait (go);
          myMpy = mpy[15:0];
          prod = 0;
          repeat (16)
            begin
                if (myMpy[0])
```

```
                    prod = prod + {mcnd, 16'h0000};
                prod = prod >> 1;
                myMpy = myMpy >> 1;
            end
        done = 1;
        wait (~go);
    end
endmodule
```

Example 2.11. The Multiply as a Separate Module.

At this point in the design process it is not possible to point to one of these solutions as being the best. Rather we can only suggest, as we have done above, why one would describe the system solely with behavioral modeling constructs ("*", function, task) or suggest structural partitioning of the behavior.

2.6 SUMMARY

The behavioral modeling statements that we have covered so far are very similar to those found in software programming languages. Probably the major difference seen so far is that the Verilog language has separate mechanisms for handling the structural hierarchy and behavioral decomposition. Functions and tasks are provided to allow for the behavior of a module to be "software engineered". That is, we can break long and sometimes repetitious descriptions into behavioral subcomponents. Separately, we can use module definitions to describe the structural hierarchy of the design and to separate concurrently operating behaviors into different modules. The examples of Section 2.5 have shown how these two approaches to modeling allow us to represent a design in a wide range of stages of completion. The next chapter continues with the topic of describing concurrent behaviors.

2.7 EXERCISES

2.1   Change the expressions containing the right shift operator in Example 2.7 to use bit and part selects and concatenations only.

2.2   Does replacing the repeat loop in Example 2.2 with the register
      declaration and **for** loop below achieve the same results?

```
reg [3:0] i;

for (i = 0; i <= DvLen; i = i+1)
   begin
      //shift and subtract statements
   end
```

2.3   Write a **for** loop statement which is equivalent to the **casez**
      statement in the following function without introducing any
      new variables.

```
function [7:0] getMask;
     input [7:0] halfVal;
     casez (halfVal)
        8'b???????1: getMask = 8'b11111111;
        8'b??????10: getMask = 8'b11111110;
        8'b?????100: getMask = 8'b11111100;
        8'b????1000: getMask = 8'b11111000;
        8'b???10000: getMask = 8'b11110000;
        8'b??100000: getMask = 8'b11100000;
        8'b?1000000: getMask = 8'b11000000;
        8'b10000000: getMask = 8'b10000000;
        8'b00000000: getMask = 8'b11111111;
     endcase
endfunction
```

3. Concurrent Process Statements

Most of the behavioral modeling statements discussed to this point have been demonstrated using single process examples. These statements are part of the body of an always statement and are repetitively executed in sequential order. They may operate on values that are inputs or outputs of the module or on the module's internal registers. In this chapter we present behavioral modeling statements that by their definition interact with activities external to the enclosing always. For instance, the *wait* statement waits for its expression to become TRUE as a result of a value being changed in another process. As in this case and the others to be presented here, the operation of the wait statement is dependent on the actions of concurrent processes in the system.

3.1 CONCURRENT PROCESSES

We have defined a process to be an abstraction of a controller, a thread of control that evokes the change of values stored in the system's registers. We conceive of a digital system as a set of communicating, concurrent processes or independent control activities that pass information among themselves. What is important is that each of these processes contains state information and that this state is altered as a function of the processes current inputs and present state.

Example 3.1 shows an abstract description of a computer. An implementation of the hardware controller for the process described in the always statement is as a sequential state machine with output and next state logic. This state machine would control a data path that includes the registers, arithmetic-logic units, and steering logic such as buses and multiplexors.

```
module computer;
    always
      begin
          power-on initializations
          forever
            begin
                fetch and execute instructions
            end
      end
endmodule
```

Example 3.1. An Abstract Computer Description.

Consider that this process may interact with another process in the system, possibly an input interface that receives bit-serial information from a video terminal. The process abstraction is necessary in this case because there are two independent, but communicating, threads of control: the computer, and the input interface. The input interface process watches for new input bits from the terminal and signals the computer when a byte of data has been received. The other process, the computer described in Example 3.1, would only interact with the input interface process when a full byte of information has been received.

These two processes could have been described as one, but it would have been quite messy and hard to read. Essentially, each statement of the computer process would have to include a check for new input data from the interface and a description of what to do if it is found. In the worst case, if we have two processes that have n and m states respectively, then the combined process with equivalent functionality would have $n*m$ states -- a description of far higher complexity. Indeed, it is necessary to conceive of the separate processes in a system and describe them separately.

However, when several processes exists in a system and information is to be passed among them, we must synchronize the processes to make sure that correct information is being passed. The reason for this is that one process does not know what state another process is in unless there is some explicit signal from that process giving such information. That is, each of the processes is asynchronous with respect to the others. For instance, they may be operating at their own clock rate, or they may be producing data at intervals that are not synchronized with the intervals when another process can consume the data. In such instances, we must synchronize the processes, providing explicit signals between them that indicate something about their internal state and that of the data shared among them.

In hardware, this synchronization is typically implemented with "data-ready" handshakes -- one process will not read the shared data until the other signals with a "data-ready" signal that new data is present -- when the other signals that the data has been read, the first unasserts the "data-ready" signal until new information is available. Synchronizing signals are typical, indeed necessary, when information is to be passed correctly among separate processes.

The statements in this chapter pertain to describing behavior that involves the interactions among concurrent processes.

3.2 EVENTS

Event control statements provide a means of watching for a *change* in a value. The execution of the process containing the *event control* is suspended until the change occurs. Thus, the value must be changed by a separate process.

It is important to note that the constructs described in this section trigger on a *change* in a value. That is, they are edge-sensitive. When control passes to one of these statements, the initial value of the input being triggered on is checked. When the value changes later (for instance, when a positive edge on the value has occurred), then the event control statement completes and control continues with the next statement.

This section covers two basic forms of the event control: one that watches for a value change, and another, called the *named event,* that watches for an abstract signal called an event.

3.2.1 Event Control Statement

We repeat Example 1.5 here to motivate the discussion of event control statements.

```
module dEdgeFF (q, clock, data);
    output  q;
    reg     q;
    input   clock, data;

    initial
        q = 0;

    always
        @(negedge clock) #10 q = data;
endmodule
```

Example 3.2. A D-Type Edge-Triggered Flip Flop.

In this example, the statement:

@(negedge clock) #10 q = data

models the negative edge triggering of a D-type flip flop. This procedural *event control* statement watches for the transition of **clock** from 1 to 0 and then delays 10 time units before assigning **q** with the value of **data**.

In addition to specifying a negative edge to trigger on, we may also specify a positive edge ("posedge") or make no specification at all. Consider:

@(z) a = b;.

Here, **a** will be loaded with the value **b** if there is any change on **z**.

The general form of the event control statement is:

@ (qualifier expression) statement;

The qualifier may be "posedge", "negedge", or it may be left blank. The expression is a gate output, wire, or register whose value is generated as a result of activity in another process. The event control begins watching for the specified change from the time procedural control passes to it. Changes prior to the time when control passed to the event control statement are ignored. After the event occurs, the statement is executed. If, while waiting for the event, a new value for the expression is generated that happens to be the same as the old value, then no event occurs.

At times, the event control expression may take on unknown values. A negative edge is defined as a transition from 1 to 0, 1 to x, or x to 0. A positive edge is defined as a transition from 0 to 1, 0 to x, or x to 1.

Any number of events can be expressed in the event control statement such that the occurrence of any one of them will trigger the execution of the statement. A time-out example is shown in Example 3.3.

```
always
    begin
        // start the timer that will produce the timeOut signal

        @(posedge inputA or posedge timeOut)
            regA = regB;
        // other statements
    end
```

Example 3.3. ORing Two Events in an Event Control Statement.

In this example, we are watching for one of two events, a positive edge on **inputA**, or a positive edge on **timeOut**. The two events are separated by the keyword **or**. This construct is important in concurrent process applications because we may find that one process could be watching for an event that will never occur. This situation, called a *deadlock*, may occur because of faulty reasoning on the part of the description writer, or because of a fault or breakdown in a working product. In this case, the input from the timer allows us to trigger on the intended event, the change on **inputA**. However, if the **InputA** event does not occur with a reasonable amount of time, the process can extricate itself from the deadlock situation and begin some form of error recovery.

3.2.2 Named Events

The event control statements described in the previous section require that a change be specified explicitly. A more abstract version of event control, the *named event*, allows a trigger to be sent to another part of the design. The trigger is not implemented as a register or wire and thus is abstract in nature. Further, if it crosses module boundaries, it requires no port specification. Other parts of the design may watch for the occurrence of the named event before proceeding.

Example 3.4 shows the Fibonacci number generator example redone using a named event to communicate between the two modules. The **topNE** module now instantiates only two modules (**fng** and **ng**); the **nandLatch** is no longer needed as the signaling between modules is done with the named event.

The always statement in module **numberGenNE** illustrates the triggering of event **ready**:

```
-> ready;
```

The event must have been previously declared as on the fourth line of the module description. After a 100 time unit delay, the always statement will increment the value **x**, trigger event **ready**, and then begin delaying for another 100 time units. Module **fibNumberGenNE** watches for the event on the first line of its always statement:

```
@ng.ready
    myValue = startingValue;
```

The name "ng.ready" is a *hierarchical name* for event **ready** and will be explained after we dispense with how the named event works. For module **fibNumberGenNE** to receive the trigger, it must first have started to execute the @event statement, and then the trigger statement in module **numberGenNE** must be executed. At this time, module **fibNumberGenNE** will continue executing with the statement **myValue = startingValue;**.

This description of the Fibonacci number generator does have a race condition in it if module **fibNumberGenNE** takes longer than 100 time units to execute the always loop. Module **numberGenNE** produces a value every 100 time units and sends a trigger. If module **fibNumberGenNE** did not get around its always loop in less than that time, it would miss **numberGenNE's** trigger. The result would be that the Fibonacci number of every other number produced by **numberGenNE** would be calculated. The Fibonacci description starting in Example 1.9 did not have this problem. Module **numberGen** and **fibNumberGen** synchronized themselves with the **nandLatch**.

```
module topNE();
    wire [15:0] number, numberOut;

    numberGenNE      ng(number);
    fibNumberGenNE fng(number, numberOut);
endmodule

module numberGenNE(number);
    output [15:0] number;
    reg    [15:0] number;
    event        ready;

    initial
      number = 3;

    always
      begin
        #100 number = number + 1;
        -> ready;                        //generate event signal
      end
endmodule

module fibNumberGenNE(startingValue, fibNum);
    input  [15:0] startingValue;
    output [15:0] fibNum;

    reg [15:0]   myValue;
    reg [15:0]   fibNum;

    always
      begin
        @ng.ready                       //accept event signal
          myValue = startingValue;
        for (fibNum = 0; myValue != 0; myValue = myValue - 1)
          fibNum = fibNum + myValue;
        $display ("%d, fibNum=%d", $time, fibNum);
      end
endmodule
```

Example 3.4. Fibonacci Number Generator Using Named Events.

Note that there is no register to hold the trigger, nor any wire to transmit it; rather it is a conceptual event which when it occurs in one module, can trigger other modules that were previously stopped at an @event statement. Further, the named event is more abstract than the event control in that no hardware implementation clues are given. That is, a posedge event control implies that some form of edge triggering logic will be used to detect that such a transition has occurred. The named event implies that the hardware designer or synthesis program can select from a number of possible implementations.

3.2.3 An Example of Hierarchical Names

The scopes of register and wire declarations, and module instance names are the module in which they are defined. The hierarchical naming mechanism, as illustrated by "ng.ready" in Example 3.4, is used to gain access to names defined in other modules. We can view the module hierarchy of the design as the tree shown in Figure 3.1 and see that in module **topNE** there is an instance of a module called **ng**. In that instance there is an event named **ready**. The syntax "ng.ready" names the event to watch for by giving its complete path name -- starting at the root of the hierarchy (in module **topNE**), going down into module **ng**, and finding event **ready**. The name **top** need not be given in the hierarchical name because **ng** is known within the root module.

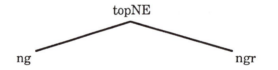

Figure 3.1. An Illustration of Hierarchical Names.

Although we can gain access to any named item in the description with this mechanism, it is more appropriate to stay within the normal scoping rules which enforce better style, readability, and maintainability. The hierarchical name in the named event was used here to show how two modules could share a named event. If we chose to model our system as one module that included two always statements, one for the behavior of **fibNumberGenNE** and the other for the behavior of **numberGenNE**, then we would not have to use the hierarchical name. The event would have been declared within the module and both always statements could have accessed it directly.

3.3 THE WAIT STATEMENT

Examples of the wait statement have already been given in several places. However, now that we have defined processes, it is instructive to discuss this statement in more detail.

The wait statement is a concurrent process statement that waits for its conditional expression to become TRUE. Conceptually, execution of the process stops until the expression becomes TRUE. By definition, the conditional expression must include at least one value that is generated by a separate, concurrent process -- otherwise, the conditional expression would never change. Because the wait must work with inputs from other processes, it is a primary means of synchronizing two concurrent processes.

The wait statement condition is level-sensitive. That is, it does not wait for a change in a value. Rather it only checks that the value of the conditional is TRUE. If it is, execution continues. If it is FALSE, the process waits.

The wait is often used in handshaking situations where we are synchronizing two processes. Example 3.5 illustrates the situation where a process will only read the **dataIn** input if the **ready** input is TRUE. The wait synchronizes the two processes by insuring that the consumer process (shown in Example 3.5) does not pass the wait statement and consume the data until the producer process generates **dataIn** and sets the **ready** signal to TRUE. The **ready** signal is a synchronization signal that tells the consumer process that the producer process has passed the state where **dataIn** is generated. In this way, the two processes become synchronized by the **ready** signal.

```
module consumer(dataIn, ready)
    input   [7:0]   dataIn;
    input           ready;
    reg     [7:0]   in;

    always
      begin
        wait (ready)
              in = dataIn;
          //...consume  dataIn
      end
endmodule
```

Example 3.5. The Consumer Module.

The general form of the wait statement is:

wait (expression) statement;

The expression is evaluated and if it is TRUE, the process proceeds to execute the statement. If it is FALSE, the process stops until it becomes TRUE. At that time, the process will proceed with the statement. Again, the change in the expression must come about from the actions of another concurrent process.

It is interesting to note that there would be a problem simulating Example 3.5 if there were no other event control or delay operations in the always statement. If this were true, then once the wait condition becomes TRUE, the loop would continue to be executed forever as the wait will never be FALSE. In one sense, this problem comes about because the simulator is simulating concurrent processes in a sequential manner and only switching between simulating the concurrent processes when a wait for a FALSE condition, delay, or event control is encountered. Since none of these are encountered in this loop, a simulation would loop forever in this always statement.

Actually, this is a more general problem in describing concurrent systems. In general, we cannot assume much about the speed of the processes in relation to each other, and thus, we need to introduce more synchronization signals to insure their correct execution. If Example 3.5 had another synchronization point, say a wait(~ready), then the producer and consumer in the example would be more tightly synchronized to each other's operating speed. Further, the simulation would also run correctly. The next section illustrates this with further examples.

3.3.1   A Complete Producer-Consumer Handshake

Example 3.5 could exhibit some synchronization errors. Specifically, the consumer never signals to the producer that the **dataIn** has been consumed. Two possible errors could occur because of this incomplete handshake:

- The producer may operate too fast and change **dataIn** to a new value before the consumer has a chance to read the previous value. Thus the consumer would miss a value.

- The consumer may operate too fast and get around its always statement and see the **ready** still TRUE. Thus it would read the same data twice.

We need to synchronize the processes so that regardless of the speed of their implementation they function correctly. One method of synchronizing two processes is with a fully-interlocked handshake as shown in Figure 3.2.

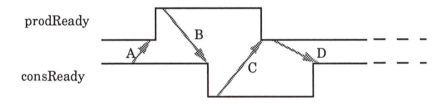

Figure 3.2. A Fully Interlocked Handshake.

The handshake illustrated above is described in Examples 3.6 - 3.8 and the following paragraphs.

At the start of the transfer, the producer of data sets producer-ready (**prodReady**) to FALSE (or zero) indicating that it is not ready to send any information. The consumer sets consumer-ready (**consReady**) to TRUE (or one) indicating that it is ready to receive information. When producer has generated a value, and it sees that **consReady** is one (arrow A in Figure 3.2), it loads the value into the output register **dataOut** and sets **prodReady** to one. It then waits for the consumer to receive the value and set **consReady** to zero. The consumer, seeing **prodReady** at level one, makes a copy of the input and sets **consReady** to zero (arrow B in Figure 3.2).

The producer now knows that the consumer has received the data so it sets **prodReady** back to zero, signalling the end of its half of the transfer (arrow C in Figure 3.2). The producer proceeds with its business and the consumer consumes the data. Then, seeing that the producer has finished its transfer, the consumer indicates that it is ready for another transfer by setting **consReady** (arrow D in Figure 3.2). The consumer then watches for the next transfer. At this point, the transfer is complete.

Note that we have introduced the **random** system function in the **producer**. This function returns a new random number each time it is called. This function is described in more detail in Appendix E.

```verilog
module consumer(dataIn, prodReady, consReady);
    input  [7:0]  dataIn;
    input         prodReady;
    output        consReady;

    reg           consReady;
    reg    [7:0]  dataInCopy;

    always
      begin
        consReady = 1;              // indicate consumer ready
        forever
          begin
            wait (prodReady)
              dataInCopy = dataIn;
            consReady = 0;    // indicate value consumed
            //...munch on data
            wait (!prodReady)           // complete handshake
              consReady = 1;
          end
      end
endmodule
```

Example 3.6 The Consumer With Fully Interlocked Handshake.

This method of transferring data between two concurrent processes will work correctly regardless of the timing delays between the processes and regardless of their relative speeds of execution. That is, because each process waits on each level of the other process' synchronization signal (i.e. the producer waits for both **consReady** and **!consReady**), the processes are guaranteed to remain in lockstep. Thus, the consumer cannot get around its always loop and quickly reread the previously transferred data. Nor, can the producer work so quickly to make the consumer miss some data. Rather, the producer waits for the consumer to indicate that it has received the data.

```
module producer(dataOut, prodReady, consReady);
    output  [7:0]  dataOut;
    output         prodReady;
    input          consReady;

    reg            prodReady;
    reg     [7:0]  dataOut,
                   temp;

    always
      begin
        prodReady = 0;              // indicate nothing to transfer
        forever
          begin
            // ... produce data and put into "temp"
            wait (consReady) // wait for consumer ready
              dataOut = $random;
            prodReady = 1;    //indicate ready to transfer
            wait (!consReady)         //finish  handshake
              prodReady = 0;
          end
      end
endmodule
```

Example 3.7. The Producer With Fully Interlocked Handshake.

```
module  ProducerConsumer;
    wire [7:0] data;
    wire       pReady, cReady;

    producer   p(data, pReady, cReady);
    consumer   c(data, pReady, cReady);
endmodule
```

Example 3.8. The Producer-Consumer Module.

The timing independence of this example is in contrast to the Fibonacci example shown in Example 3.4. In that example, the system will work correctly as long as the consumer (**fibNumGen**) can execute its loop in less than 100 time units. Often, such timing constraints are reasonable in digital system design. The complexity of the implementation is less than that of a fully-interlocked handshake. However, under certain clocking conditions and/or changed technologies, a design may no longer work. Such is life when living in the concurrent lane.

3.3.2   Comparison of the Wait and While Statements

It is incorrect to use the while statement to watch for an externally generated condition. Even though the final implementation of the state machine that waits for the condition generated by another concurrent process may be a "while" (i.e. stay in state Z while ready is FALSE), conceptually we are synchronizing separate processes and we should use the appropriate wait construct.

A further explanation of the differences between the wait and while involves the use of the simulator. Assuming a uniprocessor running a simulator, each always and initial statement is simulated as a separate process, one at a time. Once started, the simulator continues executing a process until either a delay control (#), a wait with a FALSE condition, or an event (@) statement is encountered. In the case of the delay control, event, or a wait with a FALSE condition, the simulator stops executing the process and finds the next item in the time queue to simulate. In the case of the wait with a TRUE expression, simulation continues with the same process. A while statement will never stop the simulator from executing the process.

Therefore, since the while statement shown in Example 3.9 waits for an external variable to change, it will cause the simulator to go into an endless loop. Essentially, the process that controls **inputA** will never get a chance to change it. Further, if the loop were corrected by using a wait statement in place of the while, an infinite loop would still occur. Since the wait is level sensitive, once it's condition becomes TRUE, it will continue to execute unless stopped by a wait with a FALSE condition, event control, or delay statement within the loop.

Substituting a wait statement in Example 3.9 would be correct only if the body of the loop contained either a delay, wait (FALSE), or event control. These would all stop simulation of this process and give the process that controls **inputA** a chance to change its value.

```
module endlessLoop (inputA);
   input   inputA;

   always
     begin
       while (inputA)
         ;      /* wait for external variable */
       // other statements
     end
endmodule
```

Example 3.9. An Endless Loop.

3.3.3   Comparison of Wait and Event Control Statements

In essence, both the event and wait statements watch for a situation that is generated by an external process. The difference between the two is that the event control statement is edge-triggered whereas the wait is a level-sensitive statement.

Thus the event control is appropriate for describing modules that include edge-triggering logic, such as flip flops. When active, the event statement must see a change occur before its statement is executed. We may write:

```
@(posedge clock)   statement;
```

When control passes to this statement, if clock has the value one, the execution will stop until the next transition to one. That is, the event operator does not assume that since clock is one that a positive edge must have occurred. Rather, it must see the positive edge before proceeding.

The wait, being level-sensitive, only waits if its expression is FALSE.

3.4   DISABLING NAMED BLOCKS

In Example 2.4, we showed how the *disable* statement could be used to break out of a loop or continue executing with the next iteration of the loop. The disable statement, using the same syntax, is also applicable in concurrent process situations. Essentially, the disable statement may be used to disable (or stop) the execution of any named begin-end block -- execution will then continue with the next statement following the block. The block may or may not be within the process containing the disable statement.

Module **numberGen** in Example 3.4 produces a new **number** and triggers **ready** every 100 time units. Consider the situation where we would want to reset this device asynchronously. That is, we do not want the reset to be synchronized to the 100 time unit delay period. Rather, on the negative edge of the reset input, we want the number generator to stop and begin again. Example 3.10 illustrates this behavior.

```
module numberGenDisable (number, reset);
    output  [15:0]  number;
    input           reset;
    event           ready;
    reg  [15:0]     number;

    always
       begin :generator
          number = 3;
          forever
             begin
                #100 number = number + 1;
                -> ready;
             end
       end

    always
       @(negedge reset)  disable generator;
endmodule
```

Example 3.10. Using Disable Statement to Model a Reset.

Two process statements are used to model the behavior. The first process is similar to the previous example except that the begin statement is given the name **generator**. The second process statement models the asynchronous activity of watching for the **reset** line to change to zero. When a negative edge occurs on **reset, generator** is disabled. The disable kills the named begin-end block. Since this is the only begin-end in the always statement, the always statement will restart the **generator** block again. Thus, 100 time units after the **reset** edge, the **numberGenDisable** module will produce the value 4 and trigger **ready**.

The action of the disable statement not only stops the named block, but also any functions or tasks that have been called from it. Also, any functions or tasks they have called are also stopped. Execution continues at the next statement after the block. If you disable the task (or function) you are in, then you return from the task (or function).

It is also interesting to point out what is not stopped by the disable statement. If the disabled named block has triggered an event control, by changing a value or by triggering a named event, the processes watching for these events will already have been triggered. They will not be stopped by the disable.

When we defined the term process, we emphasized that it referred to an independent thread of control. The implementation of the control was irrelevant, it could be as a microcoded controller, simple state machine, or as some other way. In the case of Example 3.10, if we assume that the first state of the controller implementing the first always statement is encoded as state zero, then the second always could be implemented as a direct edge-sensitive clear of the state register of the first always' controller. That is, the second always statement would not look like a state machine, rather it would be some simple edge-sensitive logic. The point is that regardless of the implementation of the two processes, there are two independent activities in the system capable of changing state. Each is active and operating independently of the other.

3.5 QUASI-CONTINUOUS ASSIGNMENT

The continuous assignment statement, presented in an earlier chapter, allows for the description of combinational logic whose output is to be computed anytime any one of the inputs change. There is a procedural version of the continuous assignment statement that allows for continuous assignments to be made to registers for certain specified periods of time. Since the assignment is not in force forever, as is true with the continuous assignment, we call this the *quasi-continuous assignment*.

Consider the following example of a preset and clear on a register.

```
module dFlop (preset, clear, q, clock, d)
    input   preset, clear, clock, d;
    output  q;
    reg   q;

    always
       @(clear or preset)
          begin
            if (!clear)
                #10   assign q = 0;
            else if (!preset)
                #10   assign q = 1;
            else
                #10   deassign q;
          end

    always
       @(negedge clock)
          #10   q = d;
endmodule
```

Example 3.11. Flip Flop With Quasi-Continuous Assignment.

Note first that the difference between continuous and quasi-continuous is immediately obvious from the context; the quasi-continuous assignment is a procedural statement executed only when control passes to it. (The continuous assignment is always active, changing its outputs whenever its inputs change.) In this example, the first always statement describes a process that reacts to a change in either the **clear** or **preset** signals. If **clear** became zero, then we assign register **q** to be zero. If **preset** became zero, then we assign register **q** to be one. When a change occurs and neither are zero, then we *deassign* **q** (essentially undoing the previous quasi-continuous assignment), and then **q** can be loaded with a value using the normal clock method described by the second always statement.

It is important to note that the quasi-continuous assignment overrides a normal procedural assignment to a register. Thus, even if the negative edge of the clock occurred as watched for in the second always statement, the procedural assignment of **d** to **q** would not take effect. The value quasi-continuously assigned remains in the register after the deassignment.

3.6 SEQUENTIAL AND PARALLEL BLOCKS

The begin-end blocks that we have seen so far are examples of sequential blocks. Although their main use is to group multiple procedural statements into one compound statement, they also allow for the new definition of parameters, registers, and event declarations. Thus new local variables may be specified and accessed within a begin-end block.

An alternate version of the sequential begin-end block is the parallel or fork-join block shown below. Each statement in the fork-join block is a separate process that begins when control is passed to the fork. The join waits for all of the processes to complete before continuing with the next statement beyond the fork-join block.

```
module microprocessor;
    always
      begin
        resetSequence;
        fork:   mainWork
          forever
              fetch and execute instructions;
          @(posedge reset)
              disable mainWork;
        join
      end
endmodule
```

Example 3.12. An Illustration of the Fork-Join Block.

This example illustrates the description of an asynchronous reset restarting a process. A **resetSequence** initializes registers and then begins the fork-join block named **mainWork**. The first statement of the fork is a forever loop that describes the main behavior of the microprocessor. The second statement is the process that watches for the positive edge of the **reset** signal. When the positive edge of the **reset** occurs, the **mainWork** block is disabled. As described previously, when a block is disabled, everything in the named block is disabled and execution continues with the next statement, in this case the next iteration of the always statement. Thus, no matter what was happening in the **fetch and execute** behavior of the system, the **reset** is able to asynchronously restart the whole system.

Example 3.13 shows a less abstract use of the fork-join block. Example 3.10 has been rewritten, this time with a single always that includes a fork-join.

```
module numberGenFork (number, reset);
    output [15:0] number;
    input        reset;
    event        ready;
    reg   [15:0] number;

    always
       begin
         number = 3;
         fork : generator
           begin
              #100 number = number + 1;
              -> ready;
           end
           @(negedge reset)
               disable generator;
         join
       end
endmodule
```

Example 3.13. The Fibonacci Number Generator With Reset.

Again, it is important to note that we consider each of the statements of the fork-join as a separate process. This example essentially replaced two always statements by one that has a fork-join. Comparing back to Example 3.10 serves to enforce further the notion that each statement in the fork-join should be considered, at least conceptually, a separate process.

3.7 EXERCISES

3.1 Rewrite the consumer and producer modules in Examples 3.6 and 3.7 at the behavioral level, such that a common clock signal controls the timing of the data transfer between the modules. On consecutive positive clock edges, the following is to happen: 1) the producer sets up the data on its output, 2) the consumer reads the data, 3) the producer sets up its next data value, and so on.

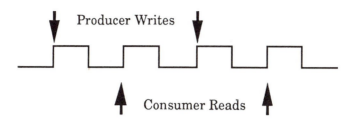

For the design to be valid there needs to be a suitable power-on initialization mechanism. Find a solution to this and include it in the model.

3.2   Write a module that is both a consumer and a producer, i.e. combine Examples 3.6 and 3.7 into one module at the behavioral level using **wait** statements. The module header is:

```
module cAndP (dataIn, prodReadyIn, consReadyIn,
                    dataOut, prodReadyOut, consReadyOut);
      input   [7:0]   dataIn;
      input           prodReadyIn;
      output          consReadyIn;
      output  [7:0]   dataOut;
      output          prodReadyOut;
      input           consReadyOut;
```

The internal data processing between the consumer and producer parts is to be a simple increment operation with a delay of 10 time units. Connect an instance of this module in a loop such that data can flow around the loop forever with data being incremented each time around. Add extra code to initialize the model for execution.

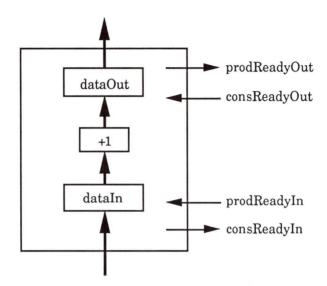

3.3 Consider four named events: **e1, e2, e3,** and **e**. Write a description to trigger event **e** after **e1, e2,** and **e3** have occurred in a strict sequence Namely, if any event goes out of order the sequence is to be reset. Then, write a description to trigger event **e** after **e1, e2,** and **e3** have each occurred three times in any order.

4. Logic Level Modeling

To this point, we have concentrated mostly on behavioral modeling of a digital system. Behavioral models are more concerned with describing the abstract functionality of a module, regardless of its actual implementation. Logic level modeling is used to model the logical structure of a module, specifying its ports, submodules, logical function, and interconnections in a way that directly corresponds to its implementation. This chapter presents the Verilog constructs that allow us to describe the logical function and structure of a system.

4.1 INTRODUCTION

There are several approaches to the logic level modeling of a digital system. Each of these approaches represents a sublevel of logic level modeling, and emphasizes different features of a module.

A *gate level* model of a circuit describes the circuit in terms of interconnections of logic primitives such as AND, OR, and XOR. Modeling at this level allows the designer to describe the actual logic implementation of a design in terms of elements found in a technology library or databook and thus be able to accurately analyze the design for such features as its timing and functional correctness. Since gate level modeling is so pervasive, the Verilog language provides *gate level primitives* for the standard logic functions.

A *structural model* of a digital system uses Verilog *module* definitions to describe arbitrarily complex elements composed of other modules and gate primitives. As we have seen in earlier examples, a structural module may contain behavioral modeling statements (an always statement), continuous assignment statements (an assign statement), module instantiations referencing other modules or gate level primitives, or any combination of these statements. By using module definitions to describe complex modules, the designer can better manage the complexity of a design. For instance, by enclosing the set of interconnected gate level primitives that implement an arithmetic-logic unit into a single module, the design description is considerably more easy to read and understand.

The *continuous assignment* statement provides a more abstract means of describing the combinational logic of a design. This approach allows for logic functions to be specified in a form similar to Boolean algebra. The continuous assignment statement typically describes the behavior of a combinational logic module, and not its implementation.

Finally, the Verilog language allows us to describe a circuit at the transistor switch level. At this level, the language provides abstractions of the underlying MOS and CMOS transistors, giving the designer access to some of the electrical characteristics of the logic implementation.

The language provides different methods for the designer to describe a system, thus allowing the description to be at the level of detail appropriate to the designer's needs. These different methods of describing the logic level function and structure of a system are presented in this and the next two chapters.

4.2 LOGIC GATES AND NETS

We start with modeling a system at the logic gate level. Verilog provides a set of 26 *gate level primitives* that have been predefined in the language. From these primitives, we build larger functional modules by interconnecting the gates with *nets* and enclosing them into modules. When describing a circuit at the gate level, we try to maintain a close (some might say strict) correspondence to the actual gate level implementation.

4.2.1 Modeling Using Primitive Logic Gates

Example 4.1 shows a structural model of a full adder using some of Verilog's gate level primitives.

```
module fullAdder(cOut, sum, aIn, bIn, cIn);
    output  cOut, sum;
    input   aIn, bIn, cIn;

    wire    x2;

    nand    (x2, aIn, bIn),
            (cOut, x2, x8);
    xnor    (x9, x5, x6);
    nor     (x5, x1, x3),
            (x1, aIn, bIn);
    or      (x8, x1, x7);
    not     (sum, x9),
            (x3, x2),
            (x6, x4),
            (x4, cIn),
            (x7, x6);
endmodule
```

Example 4.1. A One-Bit Full Adder

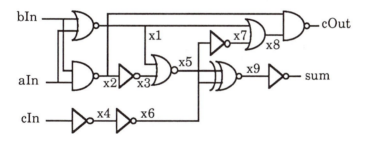

Figure 4.1. A One-Bit Full Adder.

This example was developed from a databook description of a CMOS one-bit full adder. Three single bit inputs and two single bit outputs provide connection to the outside world. Internal to the module description, we list the eleven primitive logic module instances that comprise the adder. Figure 4.1 shows a diagram of the adder with the internal connections labelled for ease of comparison. As a partial explanation, we see that there are two NAND gates, one with output x2 (note that the first parameter of a gate level primitive is its output) and inputs aIn and bIn, and the other with output cOut and inputs x2 and x8.

The general syntax for instantiating a gate is given by

gateType   strength   delay   listOfGateInstances;

where the *gateType* specifies one of the gate level primitives, the optional drive *strength* specifies the electrical characteristics of the gate's output, the optional *delay* specifies the simulation gate delay to be used with this instance, and the *listOfGateInstances* is a comma-separated list which specifies the terminals of each gate and optionally names each instance.

In Example 4.1, we have not named any of the gate instances. However, we could name the NAND gates by changing the statement to:

        nand   John (x2, aIn, bIn),
               Holland (cOut, x2, x8);

Or, we could have specified a strong0 and strong1 drive, as well as a 3 unit gate delay for each of John and Holland.

        nand   (strong0, strong1) #3
               John (x2, aIn, bIn),
               Holland (cOut, x2, x8);

The drive strength and delay specifications qualify the gate instantiation(s). When one (or both) of these qualifiers is given, then it applies to all of the defined instances in the comma-separated list. To change one or both of these qualifiers, the gate instantiation list must be ended (with a ";") and restarted. By default, the strengths of gate outputs are strong0 and strong1. Further discussion of strengths is given in Chapter 6.

A complete list of predefined gate level primitives is given in Table 4.1. For the rest of the chapter, we will concern ourselves with the bold-faced primitives. They represent logic abstractions of the transistors from which they are made. The others allow for modeling at the transistor switch level. The switch level gates will be discussed in Chapter 6.

and	**buf**	nmos	tran	pullup
nand	**not**	pmos	tranif0	pulldown
nor	**bufif0**	cmos	tranif1	
or	**bufif1**	rnmos	rtran	
xor	**notif0**	rpmos	rtranif0	
xnor	**notif1**	rcmos	rtranif1	

Table 4.1. Gate Level Primitives.

The gate primitives in the first column of Table 4.1 implement the standard logic functions listed. In the second column, the **buf** gate is a non-inverting buffer, and the **not** gate is an inverter. The **bufif** and **notif** gates provide the **buf** and **not** function with a tristate enable input. A **bufif0** drives its output if the enable is 0 and drives a high impedance if it is 1.

For the gate level primitives in the first column, the first identifier in the gate instantiation is the single output or bidirectional port and all the other identifiers are the inputs. Any number of inputs may be listed. **Buf** and **not** gates may have any number of outputs; the single input is listed last.

Although the drive strength will be discussed further in Chapter 6, it is useful to point out that a strength may only be specified only for the gates listed in the first two columns.

4.2.2 Four-Level Logic Values

The outputs of gates drive nets that connect to other gates and modules. The set of values that a gate may drive onto a net is:

0 represents a logic zero, or FALSE condition
1 represents a logic one, or TRUE condition
x represents an unknown logic value (any of 0, 1, **z,** or in a state of change)
z represents a high-impedance condition

The values 0 and 1 are logical complements of each other. The value **x** is interpreted as "either 0 or 1 or **z** or in a state of change". The **z** is a high-impedance condition. When the value **z** is present at the input of a gate or when it is encountered in an expression, the effect is usually the same as an **x** value. It should be reiterated that even the registers in the behavioral models store these four logic values on a bit-by-bit basis.

Each of the primitive gates are defined in terms of these four logic values. Table 4.2 shows the definition of an AND gate. Definitions of the other primitives may be found in Appendix C. Note that a zero on the input of an AND will force the output to a zero regardless of the other input -- even if it is **x** or **z**.

AND	0	1	x	z
0	0	0	0	0
1	0	1	x	x
x	0	x	x	x
z	0	x	x	x

Table 4.2. Four-Valued Definition of the AND Primitive.

4.2.3 Nets

Nets are a fundamental data type of the language, and are used to model an electrical connection. Except for the *trireg* net which models a wire as a capacitor that stores electrical charge, nets do not store values. Rather, they only transmit values that are driven on them by structural elements such as gate outputs and assign statements, and registers in a behavioral model.

In Example 4.1 we see a net of type wire named **x2** being declared. We could have declared it to have a delay with the following statement

```
wire     #3     x2;
```

meaning that any change of value driven on the wire from the first NAND gate instance is delayed by 3 before it is seen at the wire's terminations (which are the other NAND gate and the NOT gate). Further, the delay could include both rise and fall time specifications:

```
wire        #(3,5)  x2;
```

meaning that the transition to 1 has a 3 unit delay and the fall to 0 has a 5 unit delay.

However, we also find many more wires *declared implicitly* in Example 4.1. For instance, net **x9** which is the output of the XNOR gate has not been declared in the **fullAdder** module. If an identifier is used in a module instantiation and has not been previously declared, then the identifier is implicitly declared to be a scaler net of type wire. (By default, the type of an implicit declaration is type **wire**. However, this may be overridden by the *default_nettype typeOfNet* compiler directive where typeOfNet is any of the net types listed in Table 4.4 except the supply0 and supply1 types.)

Wire **x2** need not have been declared separately here. It was only done so for illustration purposes.

Example 4.2 illustrates the use of a different type of net, the wired-AND, or *wand*. The wired-AND performs the AND function on the net. The only difference between the AND gate and the wand is that the wand will pass a **z** on its input whereas an AND gate will treat a **z** on its input as an **x**.

```
module andOfComplements (a, b, c, d);
      input   a, b;
      output  c, d;

      wand  c;
      wire  d;

      not  (c, a);
      not  (c, b);

      not  (d, a);
      not  (d, b);
endmodule
```

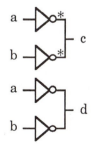

Example 4.2. Wire AND Example.

Here we illustrate the differences between the normal wire and wand net types. **d** is declared to be a wire net, and **c** is declared to be a wand net. **c** is driven by two different NOT gates as is **d**. A net declared wand will implement the wired-AND function. The output **c** will be zero if any one of the inputs to the wand net is zero (meaning that one of the inputs, **a** or **b**, was one). The output **c** will be one if both of the inputs **a** and **b** are zero.

On the other hand, **d** is a wire net driven by two gates. Its value will be unknown (**x**) unless both gates drive it to the same value. Essentially the wand allows for several drivers on the net and will implement the wired-AND function between the drivers, while the wire net will show an unknown (**x**) when different values are driven on it. Table 4.3 shows the outputs for all possible inputs to Example 4.2.

a	b	c	d	a	b	c	d
0	0	1	1	x	0	x	x
0	1	0	x	x	1	0	x
0	x	x	x	x	x	x	x
0	z	x	x	x	z	x	x
1	0	0	x	z	0	x	x
1	1	0	0	z	1	0	x
1	x	0	x	z	x	x	x
1	z	0	x	z	z	x	x

Table 4.3. Wand and Wire Results From Example 4.2.

The general form of the net declaration is:

netType   chargeStrength   range   delay   listOfNames;

netType is one of the types listed below in Table 4.4, *chargeStrength* is the charge strength that may be attached to the trireg type of net, *range* is the optional specification of bit width (default is one bit), *delay* allows for the net to have its own delay, and *listOfNames* is a comma separated list of nets that will all have the given chargeStrength, range, and delay properties.

In addition to the wire and wand net types, there are nine other net types as shown in Table 4.4.

Net Type	Modeling Usage
wire and tri	Used to model connections with no logic function. Only difference is in the name. Use appropriate name for readability.
wand, wor, triand, trior	Used to model the wired logic functions. Only difference between wire and tri version of the same logic function is in the name.
tri0, tri1	Used to model connections with a resistive pull to the given supply
supply0, supply1	Used to model the connection to a power supply
trireg	Used to model charge storage on a net. See Chapter 6.

Table 4.4. Net Types and Their Modeling Usage.

4.2.4 Module Port Specifications

A port of a module can be viewed as providing a link or connection between two items, one internal to the module instance and one external to it. We have seen numerous examples of the specification of module ports. It is useful to recap some of the do's and don't's in their specification.

First, an input or inout port cannot be declared to be of type register. Either of these ports may be read into a register using a procedural assignment statement. However, a register may only drive an inout port through a gate such as a bufif0 gate.

Secondly, each port connection is a continuous assignment of source to sink where one connected item is the signal source and the other is a signal sink. The output ports of a module are by definition connected to signal source items such as nets, registers, gate outputs, or continuous assignments internal to the module. Inout ports of a module are connected internally to gate outputs or inputs. Externally, only scaler or vector nets may be connected to a module's outputs.

Finally, we may connect to a module's ports in a way other than using the ordered list described above. We may connect to a module's ports by naming the port and giving its connection. Given the definition of module **ahh** above, we can instantiate it into another module and connect its ports by name as shown below.

```
module aboveAhh;
    wire    q, r, s;
    // other declarations

    ahh   m1 (.b(s), .a(q), .c(r));
endmodule
```

In this example, we have specified that port **b** of instance **m1** of module **ahh** will be connected to wire **s**, port **a** to wire **q**, and port **c** to wire **r**. Note that a period (".") introduces the port name defined in the module definition and that the connections may be listed in any order.

4.3   CONTINUOUS ASSIGNMENT

Continuous assignments provide a means to abstractly model combinational hardware driving values onto nets. An alternate version of the one-bit full adder in the previous section is shown using continuous assigns in Example 4.3.

```
module oneBitFullAdder(cOut, sum, aIn, bIn, cIn);
output   cOut, sum;
input    aIn, bIn, cIn;

assign    sum = aIn ^ bIn ^ cIn,
          cOut = (aIn & bIn) | (bIn & cIn) | (aIn & cIn);

endmodule
```

Example 4.3. Illustration of Continuous Assignment.

Here we show the two outputs sum and cOut being described with an assign statement. The first (sum) is the exclusive-or of the three inputs, and the second is the majority function of the three inputs.

The continuous assignment is different from the procedural assignment presented in the chapters on behavioral modeling. The continuous assignment is always active (driving a 0, 1, $\mathbf{x}$, or $\mathbf{z}$), regardless of any state sequence in the circuit. If any input to the assign statement changes at any time, the assign statement will be reevaluated and the output will be propagated. This is a characteristic of combinational logic.

The general form of the assign statement is:

assign   driveStrength   delay   listOfAssignments;

where **assign** is a keyword, the *driveStrength* and *delay* specifications are optional parts, and the *listOfAssignments* can take the form of a comma-separated list as shown in Example 4.3. The drive strength of a continuous assign can be specified for assignments to scaler nets of any type except type supply0 and supply1. For instance, the above assign could have been written as shown below:

```
assign    (strong0, strong1)
          sum = aIn ^ bIn ^ cIn,
          cOut = (aIn & bIn) | (bIn & cIn) | (aIn & cIn);
```

Here we specify that both of the continuous assignments have the default drive strength.

4.3.1   Behavioral Modeling of Combinational Circuits

The continuous assign provides a means of abstracting from a gate level model of a circuit. In this sense, the continuous assign is a form of behavioral modeling for combinational circuits. That is, we only need specify the Boolean algebra of the logic function, not its actual gate level implementation. The final gate level implementation is then left to a logic synthesis program or further designer effort.

The right-hand side expression in the assign statement may contain a function call to a Verilog function. Recall that within a function, we may have procedural statements such as case and looping statements, but not wait, @event, or #delay. Thus we may use procedural statements to describe a complex combinational logic function. For instance, a description of a multiplexor illustrates a function call in an assign.

```
module multiplexor(a, b, c, d, select, e);
    input           a, b, c, d;
    input   [1:0]   select;
    output          e ;

    assign      e = mux (a, b, c,d, select);
endmodule

function  mux;
    input           a, b, c, d;
    input   [1:0]   select;

    case (select)
        2'b00:      mux = a;
        2'b01:      mux = b;
        2'b10:      mux = c;
        2'b11:      mux = d;
        default:    mux = 'bx;
    endcase
endfunction
```

Example 4.4. Function Call From Continuous Assignment.

In this example, module multiplexor has a continuous assignment which calls function **mux**. The function uses the procedural case statement to describe the behavior of the combinational multiplexing function. If one of the case expressions match the controlling expression, then **mux** is assigned the appropriate value. If none of the first four match (e.g. there is an **x** or **z** on a **select** input), then by default, **mux** is assigned to carry the unknown value **x**.

Although the assign statement provides access to an assortment of procedural statements for behaviorally describing combinational hardware, we must be cognizant of different levels of abstraction in behavioral modeling. At a high level of abstraction we have the *process* that models sequential activity as described in Chapters 2 and 3. At that level, we are describing a situation which involves a separate thread of control and the implementation will typically have its own internal state machine watching for changes on its inputs. To model this, we would define a module with an always statement and communicate with it through module ports and with the interprocess wait and event statements. Clearly, this is not the modeling situation of Example 4.4 where we are only describing a combinational multiplexor which gates one of its inputs to its output without the need for a state machine to control it.

Rather, at a lower level of abstraction we model combinational behavior which does not contain its own internal state. Instead of using Boolean algebra to describe a multiplexor, Example 4.4 used procedural statements. The use of procedural statements in a function called from an assign merely gives us another method of describing the combinational behavior. Modeling in this way does not imply the use of a sequential state machine for implementation and should not be used when sequential activity is to be modeled.

4.3.2 Net and Continuous Assign Declarations

Continuous assign statements specify a value to be driven onto a net. A shorthand way to describe this situation which combines the net and assign definition statements is shown in Example 4.5.

```
module modXor (AXorB, a, b);
    parameter size = 8, delay = 15;

    output  [size-1:0]   AXorB;
    input   [size-1:0]   a, b;

    wire   [size-1:0]    #delay AXorB = a ^ b;
endmodule
```

Example 4.5. Combined Net and Continuous Assignment.

Here we have defined a vector wire with eight bits and an eight-bit exclusive-or of inputs **a** and **b** which drive them. The delay specifies the delay involved in the exclusive-or, not in the wire drivers.

If we had declared the wire and exclusive-or separately, as

```
wire   [size-1:0]   AXorB;
assign    #delay AXorB = a ^ b;
```

we could have assigned a separate delay of 5 to the wire drivers by substituting the statement:

```
wire    [size-1:0]  #5    AXorB;
```

When a delay is given in a net declaration as shown, the delay is added to any driver that drives the net. For example, consider the module in Example 4.6. We have defined a wand net with delay of 10 and two assign statements that both drive the net. One assign statement has delay 5 and the other has delay 3. When input **a** changes, there will be a delay of fifteen before its change is reflected at the inputs that **c** connects to. When input **b** changes, there will be a delay of thirteen.

```
module wandOfAssigns (a, b, c);
    input    a, b;
    output  c ;

    wand  #10    c ;

    assign    #5    c = ~a;
    assign    #3    c = ~b;
endmodule
```

Example 4.6. Net and Continuous Assignment Delays.

Continuous assignment statements may also be used to drive an inout port. Example 4.7 shows an example of a buffer-driver.

```
module bufferDriver (busLine, bufferedVal, bufInput, busEnable);
    inout    busLine;
    input    bufInput, busEnable;
    output  bufferedVal;

    assign      bufferedVal = busLine,
                busLine = (busEnable) ? bufInput : 1'bz;
endmodule
```

Example 4.7. Continuous Assignment to an Inout.

Here we see **busEnable** being used to select between **bufInput** driving the **busLine** and a high impedance driving the line. However, no matter what the state of **busEnable**, **bufferedVal** always follows the value of **busLine**. Thus **busLine** may be driven in an external module when **busEnable** is zero and **bufferedVal** will show its value.

4.4 PARAMETERIZED DEFINITIONS

Suppose that we wanted to use modXor shown in Example 4.5, but that we wanted a different size or delay parameter for it. Verilog provides two means of respecifying the parameters within a module. The first, using the module instantiation statement, is shown in Example 4.8.

```
module param;
    // declarations
    modXor              a(a1, b1, c1);
    modXor      #(4,5)  b(a2, b2, c2);
endmodule
```

Example 4.8. Overriding Parameter Specifications.

Within module param, we have defined two instances of the **modXor** defined in Example 4.5. Instance **a** connects to eight-bit vectors and has a delay of fifteen as specified in its module definition. However, instance **b** will be a four-bit vector and have a delay of five. That is, we are able to override the parameter definitions of a module on a per-instance basis.

The order of the overriding values follows the order of the parameter specification in the module's definition. It is not possible to skip over some parameters in a module definition and respecify the rest; either the one to be skipped over should be respecified as the default, or the parameter list should be reordered to have the parameter to be skipped over at the end of the list. For instance, instance **b** in Example 4.8 could have been specified to have size four and delay 15 (the default) with the statement:

```
    modXor    #(4) b(a2, b2, c2);
```

But, to give instance **b** the default size (eight) and a different delay (20) would require us to respecify the size too.

```
    modXor    #(8,20) b(a2, b2, c2);
```

Another approach to overriding the parameters in a module definition is to use the *defparam* statement and the hierarchical naming conventions of Verilog. This approach is shown in Example 4.9.

Using the *defparam* statement, all of the respecifications of parameters can be grouped into one place within the description. In this example, the parameters of instance **b** of module **modXor** within module **dParam** have been changed so that size is four and delay is five. This is equivalent to the respecification of Example 4.8.

```
module dParam;
    // other declarations
    modXor     a(a1, b1, c1),
               b(a2, b2, c2);
endmodule

module modXor (AXorB, a, b);
    parameter          size = 8, delay = 15;
    output  [size-1:0]   AXorB;
    input   [size-1:0]   a, b;

    wire [size-1:0]   #delay AXorB = a ^ b;
endmodule

module annotate;
    defparam
        dParam.b.size = 4,
        dParam.b.delay = 5;
endmodule
```

Example 4.9. Overriding Parameter Specification With defparam.

We could have changed only the delay of instance **b** to 20 with the defparam statement:

```
module annotate;
    defparam
        dParam.b.delay = 20;
endmodule
```

Thus, the parameters may be respecified on an individual basis.

The choice of using the defparam or module instance method of modifying parameters is a matter of personal style. Using the module instance method makes it clear at the instantiation site that new values are overriding defaults. Using the defparam method allows for grouping the respecifications in specific locations.

4.5 LOGIC DELAY MODELING

Gate level modeling is used at the point in the design process when it is important to consider the timing and functionality of the actual gate level implementation. Thus, at this point the gate and net delays are modeled, possibly reflecting the actual placement and routing of the gates and nets. In this section, we will concentrate on the logic gate primitives and specifying their timing properties for simulation.

4.5.1 A Gate Level Modeling Example

The tristate NAND latch shown in Example 4.10 illustrates the use of the bufif1 gate and detailed timing information. A diagram of the circuit is also shown in Figure 4.2.

```
module triStateLatch (qOut, nQOut, clock, data, enable);
     output  qOut, nQOut;
     input   clock, data, enable;
     tri     qOut, nQOut;

     not  #5   (ndata, data);
     nand #(3,5)    d(wa, data, clock),
                    nd(wb, ndata, clock);
     nand #(12, 15)  qQ(q, nq, wa),
                    nQ(nq, q, wb);
     bufif1 #(3, 7, 13)  qDrive (qOut, q, enable),
                    nQDrive(nQOut, nq, enable);
endmodule
```

Example 4.10. A Tristate Latch.

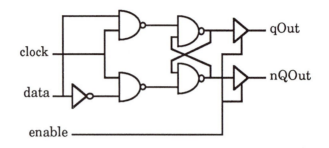

Figure 4.2. Illustration of the Tristate Latch.

This latch drives its **qOut** and **nQOut** ports, which are defined as tristate nets, when the **enable** input is one. The bufif1 gate models the tristate functionality. As shown in Table 4.5, when the control input is 1, then the output is driven to follow the input. Note that a z on the **data** input is propagated as an unknown on the data output. When the control input is 0, the output is high impedance (**z**).

		Control Input			
	Bufif1	**0**	**1**	**x**	**z**
D	**0**	z	0	L	L
A	**1**	z	1	H	H
T	**x**	z	x	x	x
A	**z**	z	x	x	x

Table 4.5. BUFIF1 Gate Function.

In the case where the control input is either **x** or **z**, the data output is modeled with **L** and **H**. **L** indicates the output is either a 0 or a **z**, and **H** indicates either a 1 or a **z**.

Other tristate modeling primitives include bufif0 which reverses the sense of the control input from bufif1, notif1 which inverts the data input and drives the output when the control input is one, and notif0 which inverts the data input and drives the output when the control input is zero. Truth tables for these gates may be found in Appendix C.

The functionality of Example 4.10 may now be described. The basic latch function is implemented by the cross-connected NAND gates **qQ** and **nQ**. When the CLOCK is low, the outputs of **d** and **nd** are held high and the latch pair hold their value. When the CLOCK is high, then the **d** and **nd** values propagate through and change the latch value. The **qQ** and **nQ** NAND gates follow the DATA input as long as the **clock** is high. The two bufif1 gates are driven by the output of the NAND latch gates and the input **enable** signal. As per the definition of the bufif1 gate, when **enable** is high, the output will be driven. When **enable** is low, the output will be **z**.

4.5.2   Gate and Net Delays

Gate, continuous assign, and net delays provide a means of accurately describing the delays through a circuit. The gate delays describe the delay from when the inputs of a gate change until when the output of the gate is changed and propagated. Continuous assign delays describe the delay from when a value on the right-side changes to when the left-hand side is changed and propagated. Net delays describe the delay from when any of the net's driving gates or assign statements change to when the value is propagated. The default delay for gates, nets, and assign statements is zero. If one delay parameter is specified, then the value is used for all propagation delays associated with the gate, net, or assign.

The following gate instantiations are excerpts from Example 4.10 and will be used to illustrate the different propagation situations.

```
not    #5    (ndata, data);
nand   #(12, 15)   qQ(q, nq, wa),
                   nQ(nq, q, wb);
bufif1 #(3, 7, 13) qDrive (qOut, q, enable),
                   nQDrive(nQOut, nq, enable);
```

Propagation delays are specified in terms of the transition to 1, the transition to 0, and the transition to **z** (turn-off delay). The NOT gate has been specified with a delay of 5. Since only this one value is given, the delay will pertain to both the transition to 1 and the transition to 0. The NAND gate instances have a rising delay of 12 and a falling delay of 15. Finally, the bufif1 gates have a rising delay of 3, falling delay of 7, and a delay to the high impedance value of 13. Note that if the gate is in the high impedance condition, then when the enable becomes 1, it will take 3 time units (i.e. the rising delay) for the output to change to 1.

Generally speaking, the delay specification takes the form of

#(d1, d2, d3)

where d1 is the rising delay, d2 the falling delay, and d3 the delay to the high impedance value. Table 4.6 summarizes the from-to propagation delay used by the simulator for the two and three delay specifications. Again, if no delay specification is made, zero is the default. If only one value is given, then all of the propagations are assumed to take that time.

A shorthand for remembering some of the delays is that a rising delay (d1) is from 0 to x, x to 1, or z to 1. Likewise, a falling delay is from 1 to x, x to 0, or z to 0.

From value	To value	2 Delays specified	3 Delays specified
0	1	d1	d1
0	x	min(d1, d2)	min(d1, d2, d3)
0	z	min(d1, d2)	d3
1	0	d2	d2
1	x	min(d1, d2)	min(d1, d2, d3)
1	z	min(d1, d2)	d3
x	0	d2	d2
x	1	d1	d1
x	z	min(d1, d2)	d3
z	0	d2	d2
z	1	d1	d1
z	x	min(d1, d2)	min(d1, d2, d3)

Table 4.6. Delay Values Used In Simulation.

The tri net defined in Example 4.10 does not include its own delay parameters. However, it could have been defined as:

tri   #(2, 3, 5)   qOut, nQOut;

In this case, any driver that drives either of these nets would incur a rising delay of 2, a falling delay of 3, and a delay to z of 5 before its output would be propagated. Thus in Example 4.10 with the bufif1 **qDrive** gate instance driving the **qOut** net, the rising delay from when an input

to gate **qDrive** changes to when the result is propagated on the **qOut** net is
5 (2 + 3), the falling delay is 10, and the delay to **z** is 18.

If the case of a continuous assign where the left-hand side is a
vector, then multiple delays are handled by testing the value of the right-
hand side. If the value was non-zero and becomes zero, then the falling
delay is used. If the value becomes **z**, then the turn-off delay is used.
Otherwise, the rising delay is used.

4.5.3   Minimum, Typical, and Maximum Delays

Verilog allows for three values to be specified for each of the rising,
falling, and turn-off delays. These values are the minimum delay, the
typical delay, and the maximum delay.

```
module IOBuffer (bus, in, out, dir);
     inout   bus;
     input   in, dir;
     output  out;

     parameter
        R_Min = 3, R_Typ = 4, R_Max = 5,
        F_Min = 3, F_Typ = 5, F_Max = 7,
        Z_Min = 12, Z_Typ = 15, Z_Max = 17;

     bufif1  #(R_Min: R_Typ: R_Max,
               F_Min: F_Typ: F_Max,
               Z_Min: Z_Typ: Z_Max)
             (bus, out, dir);

     buf     #(R_Min: R_Typ: R_Max,
               F_Min: F_Typ: F_Max)
             (in, bus);
endmodule
```

Example 4.11. Illustration of Min, Typical, and Max Delays.

Example 4.11 shows the use of the minimum, typical, and
maximum delays being separated by colons, and the rising, falling,
and turn-off delays being separated by commas. Generally, the delay
specification form

```
#(d1, d2, d3)
```

is expanded to:

```
#(d1_min: d1_typ: d1_max, d2_min: d2_typ: d2_max,
    d3_min: d3_typ: d3_max).
```

Min/Typ/Max delays may be used on gate primitives, nets, continuous assignments, and procedural assignments.

4.6   DELAY PATHS ACROSS A MODULE

It is often useful to specify delays to paths across a module (i.e. from pin to pin), apart from any gate level or other internal delays specified inside the module. The *specify block* allows for timing specifications to be made between a module's inputs and outputs. Example 4.12 illustrates the use of a specify block.

```
module dEdgeFF (clock, d, clear, preset, q);
    input   clock, d, clear, preset;
    output  q ;

    specify
      // specify parameters
      specparam    tRiseClkQ  = 100,
                   tFallClkQ  = 120,
                   tRiseCtlQ  = 50,
                   tFallCtlQ  = 60;

      // module path declarations
      (clock => q) = (tRiseClkQ, tFallClkQ);
      (clear, preset *> q) = (tRiseCtlQ, tFallCtlQ);
    endspecify

    // description of module's internals
endmodule
```

Example 4.12. Delay Path Specifications.

A specify block is opened with the *specify* keyword and ended with the *endspecify* keyword. Within the block, specparams are declared and module paths are declared. The *specparams* name constants that will be used in the module path declarations. The module path declarations list paths from the module's inputs and inouts (also called the path's *source*), to its inouts and outputs (also called the path's *destination*). The timing specified will be used for all instances of the module.

In this example, the first module path declaration specifies that the rising delay time from the **clock** input to the **q** output will be 100 time units and that the fall time will be 120. The second module path declaration specifies the delays from both **clear** and **preset** to **q**. Delay paths are not typically mixed with delay (#) operators in a module description. However, if they are, then the maximum of the two delays will be used for simulation.

Two methods are used to describe the module paths, one using "=>" and the other using "*>". The "=>" establishes a *parallel connection* between source input bits and destination output bits. The inputs and outputs must have the same number of bits. Each bit in the source connects to its corresponding bit in the destination.

The "*>" establishes a *full connection* between source inputs and destination outputs. Each bit in the source has a path to every bit in the destination. The source and destination need not have the same number of bits. In Example 4.12, we specify that **clear** and **preset** have a path to the **q** output. Multiple outputs may be specified. So, for instance, we could state:

```
(a, b *> c, d) = 10;
```

This statement is equivalent to:

```
(a => c) = 10;
(a => d) = 10;
(b => c) = 10;
(b => d) = 10;
```

Here, we assume that **a**, **b**, **c**, and **d** are single bit entities. We could also state:

```
(e => f) = 10;
```

If **e** and **f** were both 2-bit entities, then this statement would be equivalent to:

```
(e[1] => f[1]) = 10;
(e[0] => f[0]) = 10;
```

Module paths may connect any combination of vectors and scalers, but there are some restrictions. First, the module path source must be declared as a module input or inout. Secondly, the module path destination must be declared as an output or inout, and be driven by a gate level primitive other than a bidirectional transfer gate.

The delays for each path can be specified as described in the previous section, including the capability of specifying rising, falling, and turn-off delays, as well as specifying minimum, typical, and maximum delays. Alternately, six delay values may be given. Their order of specification is 0 to 1, 1 to 0, 0 to z, z to 1, 1 to z, z to 0. In addition, minimum, typical, and maximum delays may be specified for each of these.

A set of system tasks, described in the simulator reference manual, allow for certain timing checks to be made. These include, setup, hold, and pulse-width checks, and are listed within the specify block.

4.7 SUMMARY

This chapter has covered the basics in logic level modeling using the Verilog language. We have seen how to define gates and nets and interconnect them into more complex modules. The use of delays and strengths have been illustrated, and we have shown how module definitions can be parameterized. In the next two chapters we delve into the advanced topics of user-defined primitives and switch-level modeling.

4.8 EXERCISES

4.1 Write a module with the structure:

```
module progBidirect (ioA, ioB, selectA, selectB, enable);
    inout   [3:0]   ioA, ioB;
    input   [1:0]   selectA, selectB;
    input           enable;
    ...
endmodule
```

such that **selectA** controls the driving of **ioA** in the following way:

selectA	ioA
0	no drive
1	drive all 0's
2	drive all 1's
3	drive **ioB**

and **selectB** controls the driving of **ioB** in the same way. The drivers are only to be in effect if **enable** is 1. If **enable** is 0 the state of the **ioA** and **ioB** drivers must be high impedance.

A) Write this module using gate level primitives only.

B) Write this module using continuous assignments only.

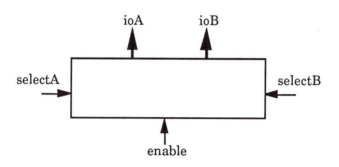

5. Defining Gate Level Primitives

Verilog provides a set of 26 gate level primitives for modeling the actual logic implementation of a digital system. From these primitives, presented in Chapter 4, larger structural models may be hierarchically described. This chapter presents an advanced method for extending the set of gate level primitives to include user-defined combinational, and level- and edge-sensitive sequential circuits.

There are several reasons for wanting to extend the set of gate level primitives. First, user-defined primitives are a very compact and efficient way of describing a possibly arbitrary block of logic. Secondly, it is possible to reduce the pessimism with respect to the unknown x value in the simulator's three valued logic, thus creating more realistic models for certain situations. Finally, simulation efficiency may be gained through their use.

5.1 COMBINATIONAL PRIMITIVES

5.1.1 Basic Features of User-Defined Primitives

As shown in Example 5.1, user-defined primitives are defined in a manner similar to a truth table enumeration of a logic function.

```
primitive carry(carryOut, carryIn, aIn, bIn);
     output  carryOut;
     input   carryIn
             aIn,
             bIn;

     table
         0  00   :   0;
         0  01   :   0;
         0  10   :   0;
         0  11   :   1;
         1  00   :   0;
         1  01   :   1;
         1  10   :   1;
         1  11   :   1;
     endtable
endprimitive
```

Example 5.1. A User-Defined Combinational Primitive.

Primitives are defined at the same lexical level as modules. i.e. primitives are not defined within modules. This example describes a primitive for generating the carry out of a single-bit full adder. **carryOut** is the output, and **carryIn, aIn,** and **bIn** are the inputs. A table is then specified showing the value of the output for the various combinations of the inputs. A colon separates the output on its right from the inputs on its left. The order of inputs in the table description must correspond to the order of inputs in the port list of the primitive definition statement. Reading from the fourth line of the table, if **carryIn** was 0, **aIn** was 1, and **bIn** was 1, then **carryOut** would be 1.

There are a number of rules that must be considered:

- Primitives have multiple input ports, but exactly one output port. They may not have bidirectional inout ports.

- The output port must be the first port in the port list.

- All primitive ports are scaler. No vector ports are allowed.

- Only logic values of 1, 0, and **x** are allowed on input and output. The **z** value cannot be specified, although on input, it is treated as an **x**.

The user-defined primitives act the same as other gate primitives and continuous assign statements. When one of their inputs changes, then the new output is determined from the table and is propagated on the output. The input values in a row of the table must correspond exactly to the values of the input ports for the row's output value to be selected. If a set of inputs appears on the ports for which there is no exact match, then the output will default to **x**. Any time delay to be associated with the primitive is specified when instances of the primitive are defined. Because primitives cannot generate the value **z**, only two delays (rising and falling) can be specified per instance.

5.1.2 Describing Combinational Logic Circuits

The usefulness of Example 5.1 might be rather low as nothing is stated about what happens when there is an unknown (**x**) input on any of the inputs. Since the table made no mention of what happens when there is an **x** input, the output of the primitive will be **x**. This is rather pessimistic in that if the other two inputs were both 1, then the output should be 1 regardless of the third input.

The table enumeration allows for the specification of 1, 0, and **x** values in its input and output sections. Further, it allows for the specification of a don't care in the table meaning that any of the three logic values are to be substituted for it when evaluating the inputs. Consider the expanded definition of the carry primitive shown in Example 5.2.

```
primitive carryX(carryOut, carryIn, aIn, bIn);
    output  carryOut;
    input   aIn,
            bIn,
            carryIn;

    table
        0  00   :  0;
        0  01   :  0;
        0  10   :  0;
        0  11   :  1;
        1  00   :  0;
        1  01   :  1;
        1  10   :  1;
        1  11   :  1;
        0  0x   :  0;
        0  x0   :  0;
        x  00   :  0;
        1  1x   :  1;
        1  x1   :  1;
        x  11   :  1;
    endtable
endprimitive
```

Example 5.2. A Carry Primitive.

Here, the last six lines of the table specify the output in the presence of unknown inputs. For instance (third line from bottom of table), if **carryIn** and **aIn** were 1, and **bIn** was **x**, then **carryOut** will be 1 regardless of the value of **bIn**. Of course, if there were two unknowns on the inputs to this gate, then the output would be unknown since there is no table entry specifying what to do in that case.

The table may be abbreviated using the **?** symbol to indicate iterative substitution of 0, 1, and **x**. Essentially, the **?** allows for us to state that we don't care what a certain value is, the other inputs will specify the output. The carry primitive example can be rewritten more compactly as shown in Example 5.3.

```
primitive carryAbbrev(carryOut, carryIn, aIn, bIn);
    output  carryOut;
    input   aIn,
            bIn,
            carryIn;

    table
        0  0?   :  0;
        0  ?0   :  0;
        ?  00   :  0;
        ?  11   :  1;
        1  ?1   :  1;
        1  1?   :  1;
    endtable
endprimitive
```

Example 5.3. A Carry Primitive With Shorthand Notation.

We can read any line of the table in two ways. Taking the first line of the table as an example, we can state that if the first two inputs are both zero, then the third input can be considered a don't care and the output will be zero. Second, we can mentally triplicate the line substituting in values of 0, 1, and **x** for the **?**. The shorthand provided by the don't care symbol improves the readability of the specification remarkably.

5.2   LEVEL- AND EDGE-SENSITIVE SEQUENTIAL PRIMITIVES

In addition to describing combinational devices, user-defined primitives may be used to describe sequential devices which exhibit level- and edge-sensitive properties. Since they are sequential devices, they have internal state that must be modeled with a register variable and a state column must be added to the table specifying the behavior of the primitive. The output of the device is driven directly by the register. The output field in the table in the primitive definition specifies the next state.

The level- and edge-sensitive primitives are harder to describe correctly because they tend to have far more combinations than normal combinational logic. This should be evident from the number of edge combinations that must be defined. Should any of the edges go unspecified, the output will become unknown (**x**). Thus, care should be taken to describe all combinations of levels and edges, reducing the pessimism.

5.2.1   Level-Sensitive Primitives

The level-sensitive behavior of a latch is shown in Example 5.4. The latch output holds its value when the **clock** is one, and tracks the input when the **clock** is zero.

```
primitive latch (q, clock, data);
     output  q ;
     reg   q ;
     input   clock, data;
     table
//      clock   data state     output
           0      1 : ? :      1;
           0      0 : ? :      0;
           1      ? : ? :      -;
     endtable
endprimitive
```

Example 5.4. A User-Defined Sequential Primitive.

Notable differences between combinational and sequential device specification are the state specification (surrounded by colons), and a register specification for the output.

To understand the behavior specification, consider the first row. When the **clock** is zero and the **data** is a one, then when the state is zero, one or **x** (as indicated by the ?), the output is one. Thus, no matter what the state is, the output (next state) depends only on the input. Line two makes a similar statement for having zero on the **data** input.

If the **clock** input is one, then no matter what the **data** input is (zero, one, or **x**) there will be no change in the output (next state). This "no change" is signified by the minus sign in the output column.

5.2.2   Edge-Sensitive Primitives

The table entries for modeling edge-sensitive behavior are similar to those for level-sensitive behavior except that a rising or falling edge must be specified on one of the inputs. It is illegal to specify more than one edge per line of the table. Example 5.5 illustrates the basic notation with the description of an edge-triggered D-type flip flop.

```
primitive dEdgeFF (q, clock, data);
    output  q ;
    reg     q ;
    input   clock, data;

    table
//     clock       data    state      output
        (01)        0      : ? :      0 ;
        (01)        1      : ? :      1 ;
        (0x)        1      : 1 :      1 ;
        (0x)        0      : 0 :      0 ;
        (?0)        ?      : ? :      - ;
          ?       (??)     : ? :      - ;
    endtable
endprimitive
```

Example 5.5. Edge-Sensitive Behavior.

The terms in parentheses represent the edge transitions of the clock variable. The first line indicates that on the rising edge of the **clock** (01) when the **data** input is zero, the next state (as indicated in the output column) will be a zero. This will occur regardless of the value of the current state. Line two of the table specifies the results of having a one at the **data** input when a rising edge occurs; the output will become one.

If the **clock** input goes from zero to don't care (zero, one, or **x**) and the **data** input and state are one, then the output will become one. Any unspecified combinations of transitions and inputs will cause the output to become **x**.

The second to the last line specifies that on the falling edge of the **clock**, there is no change to the output. The last line indicates that if the **clock** line is steady at either zero, one, or **x**, and the data changes, then there is no output change.

5.3   SHORTHAND NOTATION

Example 5.6 is another description of the edge-triggered flip flop in Example 5.5 except that this one is written using some of Verilog's shorthand notation for edge conditions.

```
primitive dEdgeFFShort (q, clock, data);
    output  q;
    reg     q;
    input   clock, data;

    table
//      clock       data state      output
          r           0  : ? :       0;
          r           1  : ? :       1;
         (0x)         0  : 1 :       1;
         (0x)         1  : 1 :       1;
         (?0)         ?  : ? :      -;
           ?          *  : ? :      -;
    endtable
endprimitive
```

Example 5.6. Edge -Sensitive Behavior With Shorthand Notation.

The symbol "r" in the table stands for rising edge or (zero to one), and "*" indicates any change, effectively substituting for "(??)". Table 5.1 lists all of the shorthand specifications used in tables for user-defined primitives.

Symbol	Interpretation	Comments
0	Logic 0	
1	Logic 1	
x	Unknown	
?	Iteration of 0, 1, and x	Cannot be used in output field
b	Iteration of 0 and 1	Cannot be used in output field
-	No change	May only be given in the output field of a sequential primitive
(vw)	Change of value from v to w	v and w can be any one of 0, 1, x, or b
*	Same as (??)	Any value change on input
r	Same as (01)	Rising edge on input
f	Same as (10)	Falling edge on input
p	Iteration of (01), (0x), and (x1)	Positive edge including x
n	Iteration of (10), (1x), and (x0)	Negative edge including x

Table 5.1. Summary of Shorthand Notation.

5.4 MIXED LEVEL- AND EDGE-SENSITIVE PRIMITIVES

It is quite common to mix both level- and edge-sensitive behavior in a user-defined primitive. Consider the edge-sensitive JK flip flop with asynchronous clear and preset shown in Example 5.7

In this example, the **preset** and **clear** inputs are level-sensitive. The **preset** section of the table specifies that when **preset** is zero and **clear** is one, the output will be one. Further, if there are any transitions (as specified by the "*") on the **preset** input and **clear** and the internal state are all ones, then the output will be one. The **clear** section of the table makes a similar specification for the clear **input**.

The table then specifies the normal clocking situations. The first five lines specify the normal JK operations of holding a value, setting a zero, setting a one, and toggling. The last line states that no change will occur on a falling edge of the **clock**.

The **j** and **k** transition cases specify that if the **clock** is a one or zero, then a transition on either **j** or **k** will not change the output.

Finally, we have the cases that reduce the pessimism of the example by specifying outputs for more situations. The first three lines include the full set of rising-edge cases, i.e. those **clock** edges including **x**. Following these, the next four lines make further specifications on when a negative edge including **x** occurs on the **clock**. Finally, the specification for **clock** having the value **x** is given. In all of these "pessimism reducing" cases, we have specified no change to the output.

There are times when an edge-sensitive and level-sensitive table entry will conflict with each other. The general rule is that when the input and current state conditions of both a level-sensitive table row and an edge-sensitive table row specify conflicting next-states, the level-sensitive entry will dominate the edge-sensitive entry. Consider the table entry in Example 5.7:

```
//clock    j k    pc    state    output
   ?       ??     01    : ? :    1;         // Case A
```

which includes the case:

```
   1       00     01    : 0 :    1;         // Case B
```

```
primitive jkEdgeFF (q, clock, j, k, preset, clear);
    output  q; reg     q;
    input   clock, j, k, preset, clear;

    table
    //clock   jk   pc    state   output
    // preset logic
        ?        ??   01    : ? :   1;
        ?        ??   *1    : 1 :   1;

    // clear logic
        ?        ??   10    : ? :   0;
        ?        ??   1*    : 0 :   0;

    // normal clocking cases
        r        00   11    : ? :   -;
        r        01   11    : ? :   0;
        r        10   11    : ? :   1;
        r        11   11    : 0 :   1;
        r        11   11    : 1 :   0;
        f        ??   ??    : ? :   -;

    // j and k transition cases
        b        *?   ??    : ? :   -;
        b        ?*   ??    : ? :   -;

    //cases reducing pessimism
        p        00   11    : ? :   -;
        p        0?   1?    : 0 :   -;
        p        ?0   ?1    : 1 :   -;
        (x0)     ??   ??    : ? :   -;
        (1x)     00   11    : ? :   -;
        (1x)     0?   1?    : 0 :   -;
        (1x)     ?0   ?1    : 1 :   -;
        x        *0   ?1    : 1 :   -;
        x        0*   1?    : 0 :   -;
    endtable
endprimitive
```

Example 5.7. A JK Flip Flop Example.

Another entry:
```
        f        ??   ??    : ? :    -;          // Case C
```

includes the case:
```
        f        00   01    : 0 :    0;          // Case D
```

Case B is a level-sensitive situation and case D is an edge-sensitive situation, but they define conflicting next state values for the same input combinations. In these two cases, the **j**, **k**, **p**, and **c** inputs are the same. Case B states that when the **clock** is one and the state is zero, then the next state is one. However, case D states that when there is a one to zero transition on the **clock** and the state is zero, then the next state is zero. But for a falling edge to be on the **clock** with the other inputs as given, the **clock** must just previously have been one and thus the next state should have already changed to one, and not zero. In all cases, the level-sensitive specification dominates and the next state will be one.

5.5   SUMMARY

The user-defined primitives represent an advanced capability in the language for specifying combinational and sequential logic primitives. The specifications are efficient and compact and allow for the reduction of pessimism with respect to the **x** value.

5.6   EXERCISES

5.1   Write combinational user defined primitives that are equivalent to: A) the predefined 3-input XOR gate, B) the equation ~((a & b) | (c & d)), and C) the multiplexor illustrated as follows:

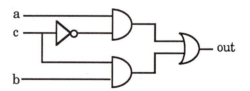

Try to reduce pessimism in the multiplexor description when the select line is unknown.

5.2   Try to reduce the pessimism in Example 5.4 for cases when the clock becomes unknown. Can more entries in Example 5.5 be given to further reduce pessimism?

5.3   Write a sequential user defined primitive of a simple two input positive edge triggered toggle flip flop with an asynchronous clear input.

5.4   Write a combinational user defined primitive of a strobed difference detector. The device is to have 3 inputs: inA, inB and strobe, such that when strobe is 1, inA is compared with inB. The output should be 0 when **inA** equals **inB**, and 1 when the comparison fails. When **inB** is unknown this indicates a don't-care situation such that regardless of the value of **inA** the output is a 0.

5.5 Develop a gate level description of an edge-sensitive JK flip flop with asynchronous clear and preset, and compare it against the user defined primitive in Example 5.7 with respect to pessimism from the unknown value.

6. Switch Level Modeling

Designs at the logic level of abstraction, describe a digital circuit in terms of primitive logic functions such as OR, and NOR, etc., and allow for the nets interconnecting the logic functions to carry 0, 1, x and z values. At the analog-transistor level of modeling, we use an electronic model of the circuit elements and allow for analog values of voltages or currents to represent logic values on the interconnections.

The switch level of modeling provides a level of abstraction between the logic and analog-transistor levels of abstraction, describing the interconnection of transmission gates which are abstractions of individual MOS and CMOS transistors. The switch level transistors are modeled as being either on or off, conducting or not conducting. Further, the values carried by the interconnections are abstracted from the whole range of analog voltages or currents to a small number of discrete values. These values are referred to as signal *strengths*.

6.1   A DYNAMIC MOS SHIFT REGISTER EXAMPLE

We began our discussion of logic level modeling in Chapter 4 by listing the primitive set of gates provided by the Verilog language (the list is reproduced as Table 6.1). At the time, only the logic level primitives were discussed. We can see from the switch level primitives, highlighted in bold in the table, that they all model individual MOS/CMOS transistors.

and	buf	nmos	tran	pullup
nand	not	pmos	tranif0	pulldown
nor	bufif0	cmos	tranif1	
or	bufif1	rnmos	rtran	
xor	notif0	rpmos	rtranif0	
xnor	notif1	rcmos	rtranif1	

Table 6.1. Gate Level Primitives.

Figure 6.1 illustrates the differences in modeling at the switch and logic levels. The circuit is a three stage, inverting shift register controlled by two phases of a clock. The relative timing of the clock phases is also shown in the figure. The Verilog description is shown in Example 6.1.

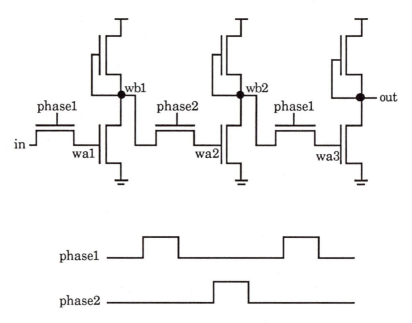

Figure 6.1. MOS Shift Register and Clock Phases.

```
//Dynamic MOS serial shift register circuit description
module shreg (out, in, phase1, phase2);
        /* IO port declarations, where 'out' is the inverse
        of 'in' controlled by the dual-phased clock */

        output  out;       //shift register output
        input   in,        //shift register input
                phase1,    //clocks
                phase2;

        tri    wb1, wb2, out;  //tri nets pulled up to VDD
        pullup //depletion mode pullup devices
                (wb1), (wb2), (out);

        trireg (medium) wa1, wa2, wa3;    //charge storage nodes

        supply0    gnd;    //ground supply

        nmos #3    //pass devices and their interconnections
                a1(wa1,in,phase1), b1(wb1,gnd,wa1),
                a2(wa2,wb1,phase2), b2(wb2,gnd,wa2),
                a3(wa3,wb2,phase1), gout(out,gnd,wa3);
endmodule
```

Example 6.1. MOS Shift Register.

The circuit consists only of nmos transistors and depletion mode pullup transistors interconnected by nets of type tri and trireg. *tri* nets model tristate nets. In this example, tri nets **wb1, wb2**, and **out** are pulled up to VDD through the declaration of three unnamed pullup gates.

Three trireg nets, **wa1, wa2**, and **wa3**, are declared. Trireg nets are different from other types of nets in that they store a value when all gates driving the net have turned off. That is, a driver can drive them (i.e. charge them) and then turn off. The value driven will remain on the trireg net even though it is no longer being driven. These nets are used in this example to model the dynamic storage of the shift register stages. The declaration of the nets shows them being given the *medium* capacitor strength (which also happens to be the default).

A net of type supply0 is defined and named **gnd**, modeling a connection to the ground terminal of the power supply. Finally, the nmos pass transistors are instantiated and connected, completing the shift register definition.

It is instructive to evoke the inputs to the shift register model and follow its simulation output. The module in Example 6.2 instantiates a copy of the **shreg** module described in Example 6.1, drives its inputs and monitors its outputs. Table 6.2 lists the output from the simulation of this example.

```
module waveShReg;
      wire    shiftout;      //net to receive circuit output value
      reg     shiftin;       //register to drive value into circuit
      reg     phase1,phase2;  //clock driving values

      parameter d = 100;  //define the waveform time step

      shreg   cct (shiftout, shiftin, phase1, phase2);

      initial
        begin :main
          shiftin = 0;    //initialize waveform input stimulus
          phase1 = 0;
          phase2 = 0;
          setmon;    // setup the monitoring information
          repeat(2)   //shift data in
            clockcct;
        end

task setmon;         //display header and setup monitoring
      begin
        $display("           time  clks  in  out  wa1-3  wb1-2");
        $monitor ($time,,,,phase1, phase2,,,,,,shiftin,,,, shiftout,,,,,
           cct.wa1, cct.wa2, cct.wa3,,,,,cct.wb1, cct.wb2);
      end
endtask

task clockcct;              //produce dual-phased clock pulse
      begin
        #d phase1 = 1;   //time step defined by parameter d
        #d phase1 = 0;
        #d phase2 = 1;
        #d phase2 = 0;
      end
endtask
endmodule
```

Example 6.2. Simulating the MOS Shift Register.

Module **waveShReg** initializes **shiftin**, **phase1**, and **phase2** to zero, prints a header line for the output table, and then sets up the monitoring of certain nets within instance **cct** of module **shreg**. Note that the nets within instance **cct** are referenced with the hierarchical naming convention (e.g. "cct.wb1"). The **clockcct** task is executed twice, evoking actions within the shift register. After two iterations of **clockcct**, the simulation is finished.

Table 6.2 lists the output from the simulation. Initially, the outputs are all unknown. After 100 time units the **phase1** clock is set to one. This enables the pass transistor to conduct and the zero value at the input to be driven onto trireg net **wa1** after one gate delay. After one more gate delay, tri net **wb1** becomes one because transistor **b1** is cutoff and **wb1** is connected to a pullup. No more gate action occurs until the **phase1** clock goes to zero at time 200. At this point, we see the value on trireg net **wa1** persisting even though there is no driver for that net (Charge stored on a trireg net does not decay with time). The **phase2** clock then becomes 1 and the value on **wb1** is transferred to **wa2**, driving transistor **b2** and net **wb2** to zero. **Phase2** is lowered and **phase1** is raised, shifting the bit to **wa3**, making the complement of the original input available at the output.

time	clks	in	out	wa1-3	wb1-2
0	00	0	x	xxx	xx
100	10	0	x	xxx	xx
103	10	0	x	0xx	xx
106	10	0	x	0xx	1x
200	00	0	x	0xx	1x
300	01	0	x	0xx	1x
303	01	0	x	01x	1x
306	01	0	x	01x	10
400	00	0	x	01x	10
500	10	0	x	01x	10
503	10	0	x	010	10
506	10	0	1	010	10
600	00	0	1	010	10
700	01	0	1	010	10

Table 6.2. Results of Simulating the MOS Shift Register.

6.2   SWITCH LEVEL MODELING

Switch level modeling allows for the *strength* of a driving gate and the size of the capacitor storing charge on a trireg net to be modeled. This capability provides for more accurate simulation of the electrical properties of the transistors than would a logic simulation.

6.2.1   Strength Modeling

Consider the description of a static RAM cell shown in Example 6.3 and Figure 6.2. Among other declarations, two NOT gates are instantiated, each with a "pull" drive strength; *pull0* for the zero output strength, and *pull1* for the one output strength. The pull drive strength is one of the possible strengths available in Verilog. It is weaker than the default *strong* drive which models a typical active drive gate output.

In the example, the two NOT gates form a feedback loop that latches a value driven on **w4** through the tranif1 gate. The *tranif1* gate is a transfer gate that conducts when its control input (**address** in this case) is one, and is nonconducting otherwise. The bufif1 gate is the read/write control for the circuit. In read mode, the bufif1 control line (**write**) is zero and its output is high impedance. When the cell is addressed, the value in the latch is connected to the output buffer **g5**. In write mode when the cell is addressed, the bufif1 gate drives **w4** through the tranif1 gate, possibly changing the latch's state.

```
//description of a MOS static RAM cell
module sram(dataOut, address, dataIn, write);
    output  dataOut;
    input   address, dataIn, write;

    tri     w1, w3, w4, w43;

    bufif1
       g1(w1, dataIn, write);
    tranif1
       g2(w4, w1, address);
    not (pull0, pull1)
       g3(w3, w4), g4(w4, w3);
    buf
       g5(dataOut, w1);
endmodule
```

```
//waveform for testing the static RAM cell
module wave_sram;
    wire dataOut;
    reg   address, dataIn, write;

    //make the sram a submodule and define the interconnections
    sram cell(dataOut, address, dataIn, write);

    //define the waveform to drive the circuit
    parameter d = 100;
    initial
      begin
        #d dis;
        #d address = 1;
        #d dis;
        #d dataIn = 1;
        #d dis;
        #d write = 1;
        #d dis;
        #d write = 0;
        #d dis;
        #d write = 'bx;
        #d dis;
        #d address = 'bx;
        #d dis;
        #d address = 1;
        #d dis;
        #d write = 0;
        #d dis;
      end

task dis;        //display the circuit state
    $display($time,,
    "addr=%v d_in=%v write=%v d_out=%v",
        address, dataIn, write, dataOut,
        " (134)=%b%b%b  w134=%v %v %v",
        {cell.w1, cell.w3, cell.w4},
        cell.w1, cell.w3, cell.w4);
endtask
endmodule
```

Example 6.3. A Static RAM Cell.

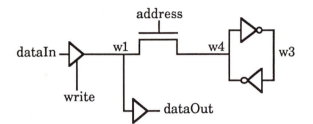

Figure 6.2. A Static RAM Cell.

time	addr	d_in	wr	d_out	134	Comments
100	x	x	x	x	xxx	
300	1	x	x	x	xxx	
500	1	1	x	x	xxx	
700	1	1	1	1	101	write function
900	1	1	0	1	101	read function
1100	1	1	x	1	101	
1300	x	1	x	x	x01	ram holds value
1500	1	1	x	1	101	
1700	1	1	0	1	101	read function

Table 6.3. Results of Simulating Static RAM.

Example 6.3 also shows a Verilog module that will evoke the **sram** module and print out the state of the nets in the circuit. The output is shown in Table 6.3 in a tabular form. The method of modeling in this example shows us a static view of the circuit; values are printed out after the "minor" gate changes have occurred.

Note first that all values in the circuit start at **x**. By time 500, the **dataIn** and **address** value are both 1. The tranif1 gate will transfer values in both directions. The bufif1 gate, having an **x** on its control input, is driving its output to level **H** (meaning 1 or **z**). Since this table only shows the Boolean values (as specified with the %b in the $display statement) we see an **x** on the bufif1 output **w1**.

At time 700, the **write** line has been one for 100 time units, driving **w1** and **dataOut** to a one. Since the tranif1 gate is conducting, **w1** and **w4** are connected. At this point, we have gate **g4** (the NOT gate) and **g1** (the bufif1 gate) both driving these connected lines. However, since **g4** has been defined to have driving strength *pull0* and *pull1* in the zero and one states respectively, its drive strength is not as strong as the buif gate which has the default *strong* drive strengths. In this case, the strong drive overwhelms the pull drive and **w4** follows **w1**, and **w3** becomes the complement. **w3** on the input to **g4** then completes the changing of the ram cell value.

At time 900, the **write** line is at zero, but the **address** line still selects the cell. This is the read function of the **sram** module; the **dataOut** indicates the saved state.

At time 1300, both **address** and **write** are **x**, and thus so is **w1** and **dataOut**. However, the **sram** still holds its value. By time 1700, **address** and **write** indicate the read function and the value stored earlier is again conducted through the tranif1 gate to the **dataOut**.

6.2.2 Strength Definitions

The above example showed two of the levels of strength available in modeling switch level circuits; Table 6.4 is a complete list. Again we can see that the strong drive of the bufif1 gate is stronger than the pull drive of the NOT gate.

There are four driving strengths and three charge storage strengths. The driving strengths are associated with gate and continuous assignment outputs, and the charge storage strengths are associated with the trireg net type. The strengths may be associated with either a 1, 0, or **x** value. That is, a gate may drive a weak zero, a weak one, or a weak **x**. The declaration abbreviation should be used with a zero or one (e.g. pull0) when gate instances and strengths are declared. The printed abbreviation column indicates how the strength is printed when the %v format is used (see later examples).

Strengths associated with gate instances and assign statements are specified within parentheses as shown:

gateType (0-Strength, 1-Strength) #(delay) instance(s);

or

assign (0-Strength, 1-Strength) #(delay) assignment(s);

Strength Name	Strength Level	Element Modeled	Declaration Abbreviation	Printed Abbreviation
Supply Drive	7	Power supply connection	supply	Su
Strong Drive	6	Default gate and assign output strength	strong	St
Pull Drive	5	Gate and assign output strength	pull	Pu
Large Capacitor	4	Size of trireg net capacitor	large	La
Weak Drive	3	Gate and assign output strength	weak	We
Medium Capacitor	2	Size of trireg net capacitor	medium	Me
Small Capacitor	1	Size of trireg net capacitor	small	Sm
High Impedance	0	Not applicable	highz	Hi

Table 6.4. Strength Specifications.

If the strengths are not given, then strong drives are assumed. Only the gate types shown in Table 6.5 support drive strength specifications:

and	or	xor	buf	bufif0	bufif1	pullup
nand	nor	xnor	not	notif0	notif1	pulldown

Table 6.5. Gate Types Supporting Drive Strength Specifications

6.2.3 An Example Using Strengths

We now look more closely at Example 6.3 and observe the gate strengths as they are calculated and printed. The $display statement:

```
$display ($time,,
    "address=%b dataIn=%b write=%b dataOut=%b",
        address, dataIn, write, dataOut,
    "(134)=%b%b%b",
        cell.w1, cell.w3, cell.w4,
    " w134=%v %v %v",
        cell.w1, cell.w3, cell.w4);
```

prints the w134 signals as binary numbers, using the %b control, and then as strengths, using the %v control. Table 6.6 shows the strengths printed out when using this statement.

time	addr	d_in	write	d_out	(134)	w134			Comments
100	StX	StX	StX	StX	xxx	StX	PuX	StX	
300	St1	StX	StX	StX	xxx	StX	PuX	StX	
500	St1	St1	StX	StX	xxx	56X	PuX	56X	
700	St1	St1	St1	St1	101	St1	Pu0	St1	Write function
900	St1	St1	St0	St1	101	Pu1	Pu0	Pu1	Read function
1100	St1	St1	StX	St1	101	651	Pu0	651	
1300	StX	St1	StX	StX	x01	StH	Pu0	651	
1500	St1	St1	StX	St1	101	651	Pu0	651	
1700	St1	St1	St0	St1	101	Pu1	Pu0	Pu1	Read function

Table 6.6. Simulation Results Showing Strengths.

The strength outputs in Table 6.6 have one of two formats. If a strength is listed with a value, then the net is being driven by that value with the specified strength. The printing abbreviations for the strengths are listed in Table 6.4. Thus **St1** indicates a strong 1, **StH** indicates a strong 1 or **z**, **Pu0** indicates a pull 0, and **PuX** indicates a driver of strength pull driving an **x**. If two numbers are given with the value, then the net is being driven by multiple sources and the numbers indicate the minimum and maximum strength levels (see level

numbers in Table 6.4) driving the net. For instance, at time 1100, net
w1 is being driven by a strong (6) and pull (5) value one.

At time 100, all of the nets have unknown values on them, but notice
that there is a strength associated with each of them corresponding to
their driver's declaration. Thus, **address, dataIn, write, w1,** and
dataOut are all strong-strength signals, whereas **w3** is a pull strength.
w4 is connected to **g4** which is a pull-strength gate and to the tranifl
gate. Since it is connected to more than one gate output, we would have
expected to see a range of strengths driven on it. Indeed this could be the
case. However, it is not the tranifl gate driving **w4**. Rather it is the
bufifl gate driving **w4** through the tranifl. The MOS gates do not have
their own drive strength. They merely propagate the values and
strengths at their input (with a possible reduction in strength depending
on gate type and strength input).

At time 500, we see net **w1** listed as 56X, indicating that it is being
driven by both a pull **x** and strong 1 driver. This indication arises
because the bufifl gate (strong) is driving an **H** (its control line is **x**)
and the tranifl gate is passing a pull-strength **x** from gate **g4**. The two
combine to drive an **x** on **w1**. Since **w1** and **w4** are connected together
through the tranifl gate, they both have the same indication.

Following the operation of the sram at time 700, we see again that the
strong strength of the bufifl gate transmitted through the tranifl gate
overrides the value driven by **g4** onto **w4**, thus allowing for a new value
to be saved. At 1300, we see that even when **address** and **write** become
unknown, the **sram** still holds its value.

6.2.4   Resistive MOS Gates

The MOS gates can be modeled as either resistive or nonresistive
devices. Nonresistive gates (nmos, pmos, cmos, tran, tranif0, and
tranifl) do not effect the signal strength from input to output (i.e.
between bidirectional terminals) except that a supply strength will be
reduced to a strong strength. In addition, pullup and pulldown gates
drive their output with a pull strength. However, when the resistive
model is used (rnmos, rpmos, rcmos, rtran, rtranif0, rtranifl), then a
value passing through the gate undergoes a reduction in drive strength
as enumerated in Table 6.7

Input Strength	Reduced Strength
Supply Drive	Pull Drive
Strong Drive	Pull Drive
Pull Drive	Weak Drive
Weak Drive	Medium Capacitor
Large Capacitor	Medium Capacitor
Medium Capacitor	Small Capacitor
Small Capacitor	Small Capacitor
High Impedance	High Impedance

Table 6.7. Strength Reduction Through Resistive Transfer Gates.

Consider another change in the **sram** specification where the tranif1 gate is declared to be a resistive transfer gate, *rtranif1*, with the following statement:

```
rtranif1
    g2(w4, w1, address);
```

Then with the detailed display statement shown in Example 6.3, we obtain the following simulation results:

time	addr	d_in	write	d_out	(134)	w134			Comments
100	StX	StX	StX	StX	xxx	StX	PuX	StX	
300	St1	StX	StX	StX	xxx	StX	PuX	StX	
500	St1	St1	StX	StX	xxx	36X	PuX	PuX	
700	St1	St1	St1	St1	1xx	St1	PuX	PuX	Write
900	St1	St1	St0	StX	xxx	WeX	PuX	PuX	Read
1100	St1	St1	StX	StX	xxx	36X	PuX	PuX	
1300	StX	St1	StX	StX	xxx	36X	PuX	PuX	
1500	St1	St1	StX	StX	xxx	36X	PuX	PuX	
1700	St1	St1	St0	StX	xxx	WeX	PuX	PuX	Read

Table 6.8. Simulation Showing Strength Reduction.

Considering the values and strengths at time 500, we now see that **w1** and **w4** are different because they are separated by a resistive device. On **w1** there is a 36x, the 6 arises from the bufif1 output driving a strong logic one and the 3 arises from **g4** driving a logic zero as reduced from a pull drive (5) to a weak drive (3) by the rtranif1 gate.

It is important to note that this version of the **sram** does not work! The previous versions of the **sram** changed the stored value because the strong output of the bufif1 gate overpowered the pull output of **g4**. But in this case, the rtranif1 gate reduces the strong output to a pull output which does not overpower the output of **g4**. Thus, **g3** does not change its output and the latching mechanism comprised of **g3** and **g4** does not capture the new value.

6.3 AMBIGUOUS STRENGTHS

A possible way of representing a scaler net value is with two bytes of information; the first byte indicates the strength of the 0 portion of the net value, and the second byte indicates the strength of the 1 portion. The bit positions within each byte are numbered from most significant down to least significant. The bit position corresponds to the strength level values as given in Table 6.4. The higher place value positions correspond to higher strengths. These are illustrated in Figure 6.3

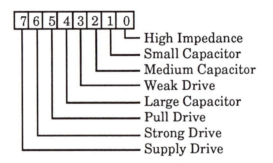

Figure 6.3. Bit Ordering For Strength Modeling.

When a logic gate is simulated, the value on its input in terms of zero, one, **x**, and **z** is determined from the strength bytes. If the zero[th] bit in either of the bytes is set when the rest of the bits are zero, or both bytes are zero, then the input is **z**. If the zero[th] bits of both bytes are zero, then for known values only one of these bytes will be non-zero. For unknown (**x**) values, both bytes will be non-zero.

Ambiguous situations arise when multiple gates drive a common net, and in situations where there is an unknown value driving a tristate control input. These situations are modeled by the net taking on a range of values, i.e. contiguous bits in the two strength bytes are set.

6.3.1   Illustrations of Ambiguous Strengths

We will list a few examples to illustrate the reasoning process. Imagine the two bytes joined together as shown in Figure 6.4

0-Strength   1-Strength

7	6	5	4	3	2	1	0	7	6	5	4	3	2	1	0

Figure 6.4. Two Strength Bytes End-to-End.

Consider the following examples where two outputs drive the same net. The representation used for the 0-strength and 1-strength bytes in the examples is that shown in Figure 6.4.

<0-strength:1-strength>=logic value.

Both the 0- and 1-strength bytes are given in binary notation. The logic value corresponding to each of the two strength bytes is given as one of 0, 1, **x,** or **z**.

```
0100_0000:0000_0000 =0    output1
0000_0000:0010_0000 =1    output2
0100_0000:0000_0000 =0    result on net
```

In the above case, output 1 is a strong zero and output 2 is a pull 1. The result on the net is a zero due to the strong driver.

```
0000_0000:0110_0000 =1    output1
0110_0000:0000_0000 =0    output2
0111_1111:0111_1111 =x    result on net
```

In this case, each output has an ambiguous strength, listed here as being both strong and pull. When these two outputs, one driving a one and the other driving a zero, are combined on the net, the result is an **x**. All the bits between the values are set as shown in the result.

```
0000_0000:0010_0000 =1   output 1
0000_0111:0111_1111 =x   output 2
0000_0000:0110_0000 =1   result on net
```

In the above case, a pull 1 and an unknown with ambiguous strengths both drive the net. The drives range from a zero of medium capacitor (2) strength through a strong one. The result is a one with ambiguous strengths ranging between strong and pull.

6.3.2   The Underlying Calculations

The above illustrations were meant to give an intuitive feel for the operation of the simulator in the presence of ambiguous strengths. In this section we present portions of the **miniSim** example shown in full detail in Chapter 7. The **miniSim** is a Verilog description of a very simple simulator that handles strengths. We will present only the portions of the Verilog description that do the strength calculations.

```
`define Val0 3'd0
`define Val1 3'd1
`define ValX 3'd2
// Convert a full strength value to a three-valued logic (0, 1 or X)
function [1:0] log3;
input [15:0] inVal;
    begin
        casez (inVal)
            16'b00000000_00000000: log3 = `ValX;
            16'b???????0_00000000: log3 = `Val0;
            16'b00000000_???????0: log3 = `Val1;
            default: log3 = `ValX;
    end
endfunction
```

Example 6.4. The log3 Function.

Example 6.4 illustrates the **log3** function which is called when a gate input is evaluated. The function converts the value **inVal** specified with two strength bytes into a three-valued logic. In the description, the first strength byte is the zero byte and the second is the one byte. The first **casez** expression says that if none of the strength bits are set, then the value is a **x**. The second expression states that if only some of the zero strength bits are one, the value is a zero. Next, if only some of the one strength bits are one, the value is a one. If none of the above conditions hold, the value is unknown.

We see two new constructs here. The first is the `define compiler directive which provides a macro capability. Whereas the *parameter* statements that we used previously can only be used to give constant numeric values to names, `define provides a general textual substitution capability. Secondly, we see how the underscore ("_") can be used in numeric values to improve readability.

The above function would be used when gates are evaluated. Example 6.5 illustrates a task used to simulate a NAND gate.

```
// Evaluate a 'Nand' gate primitive.
task evalNand;
     input fanout; //first or second fanout indicator
     begin
        storeInVal(fanout);
        // calculate new output value
        in0 = log3(in0Val[evalElement]);
        in1 = log3(in1Val[evalElement]);
        out = ((in0 == `Val0) || (in1 == `Val0)) ?
           strengthVal(`Val1) :
           ((in0 == `ValX) || (in1 == `ValX)) ?
             strengthVal(`ValX):
             strengthVal(`Val0);
        // schedule if output value is different
        if (out != outVal[evalElement])
             schedule(out);
     end
endtask
```

Example 6.5. The evalNand Task.

Although we will not describe all of the details of the task, we will describe enough to give the basic understanding of the simulation. First we call the **storeInVal** task to store the input values to this element in the global memories **in0Val** and **in1Val**. We then convert these strength values into three-valued logic and store them in **in0** and **in1**. Next, **out** is set as per the three-valued NAND of the two values. Finally, if there was a change in **out**, then we **schedule** the output to change.

Consider evaluating a wire which is driven by two inputs as shown in Example 6.6. This example parallels the above **evalNand** task, except that within the task, we deal with the strengths.

```
// Evaluate a wire with full strength values
task  evalWire;
      input        fanout;
      reg  [7:0] mask;
      begin
        storeInVal(fanout);

        in0 = in0Val[evalElement];
        in1 = in1Val[evalElement];
        mask = getMask(in0[15:8]) & getMask(in0[7:0]) &
           getMask(in1[15:8]) & getMask(in1[7:0]);
        out = fillBits((in0 | in1) & {mask, mask});

        if (out != outVal[evalElement])
           schedule(out);
        if (DebugFlags[2])
           $display(
    "in0 = %b_%b\nin1 = %b_%b\nmask= %b %b\nout = %b_%b",
           in0[15:8],in0[7:0], in1[15:8],in1[7:0],
           mask,mask, out[15:8],out[7:0]);
      end
   endtask
```

Example 6.6. The evalWire Task.

Specifically, function **getMast**, shown in Example 6.7, is called to develop a mask for the final result and function **fillBits**, shown in Example 6.8, actually constructs the strength bytes for the result.

```
// Given either a 0-strength or 1-strength half of a strength value
// return a masking pattern for use in a wire evaluation.
function [7:0] getMask;
    input [7:0] halfVal; //half a full strength value

    casez (halfVal)
        8'b???????1: getMask = 8'b11111111;
        8'b??????10: getMask = 8'b11111110;
        8'b?????100: getMask = 8'b11111100;
        8'b????1000: getMask = 8'b11111000;
        8'b???10000: getMask = 8'b11110000;
        8'b??100000: getMask = 8'b11100000;
        8'b?1000000: getMask = 8'b11000000;
        8'b10000000: getMask = 8'b10000000;
        8'b00000000: getMask = 8'b11111111;
    endcase
endfunction
```

Example 6.7. The getMask Function.

Let's consider the following example presented in the previous section. In this case, we have ambiguous strengths on both outputs driving the wire.

```
0000_0000:0110_0000 =1    output 1 -- in0
0110_0000:0000_0000 =0    output 2 -- in1
0111_1110:0111_1110 =x    result on net
```

Following along in task **evalWire**, we see that **in0** and **in1** are each loaded with the two strength bytes for the inputs to the wires. A mask is generated by calling **getMask** four times, each with a different strength byte. The results are ANDed together and put in **mask**. The results, in order, are:

```
1111_1111
1110_0000
1110_0000
1111_1111
1110_0000          mask
```

```
//Given an incomplete strength value, fill the missing strength bits.
// The filling is only necessary when the value is unknown.
function [15:0] fillBits;
input [15:0] val;
  begin
    fillBits = val;
    if (log3(val) == `ValX)
    begin
      casez (val)
16'b1???????_????????: fillBits = fillBits | 16'b11111111_00000001;
16'b01??????_????????: fillBits = fillBits | 16'b01111111_00000001;
16'b001?????_????????: fillBits = fillBits | 16'b00111111_00000001;
16'b0001????_????????: fillBits = fillBits | 16'b00011111_00000001;
16'b00001???_????????: fillBits = fillBits | 16'b00001111_00000001;
16'b000001??_????????: fillBits = fillBits | 16'b00000111_00000001;
16'b0000001?_????????: fillBits = fillBits | 16'b00000011_00000001;
      endcase
      casez (val)
16'b????????_1???????: fillBits = fillBits | 16'b00000001_11111111;
16'b????????_01??????: fillBits = fillBits | 16'b00000001_01111111;
16'b????????_001?????: fillBits = fillBits | 16'b00000001_00111111;
16'b????????_0001????: fillBits = fillBits | 16'b00000001_00011111;
16'b????????_00001???: fillBits = fillBits | 16'b00000001_00001111;
16'b????????_000001??: fillBits = fillBits | 16'b00000001_00000111;
16'b????????_0000001?: fillBits = fillBits | 16'b00000001_00000011;
      endcase
    end
  end
endfunction
```

Example 6.8. The fillBits Function.

Two copies of mask concatenated together are then ANDed with the
result of ORing the inputs **in0** and **in1** together.

```
0110_0000:0110_0000        OR of in0 and in1
1110_0000:1110_0000        mask, mask
0110_0000:0110_0000        result passed to fillBits
```

This result is passed to **fillBits** which will determine that this value is **x**
and will then execute the two casez statements. In the first casez,
fillBits will be set to 0111_1111:0110_0000, and the second casez will OR
in the value 0000_0000:0111_1111. **fillBits** will have the final value:

0111_1111:0111_1111.

This result, if different from the previous value on the wire, is scheduled.

6.4 SUMMARY

We have seen in this section how strengths may be assigned to gate outputs and assign statements, and how logic values driven at these strengths may be propagated through gates, driven on nets, and stored on trireg nets. The chapter closed with a brief discussion of the **miniSim**, a simulator written in the Verilog language that demonstrates how the logic strengths are combined together. The whole **miniSim** example is left to Chapter 7.

6.5 EXERCISES

6.1 Change the method of monitoring in Example 6.2 to that of strobing the signals 1 time unit before the positive edge of the **phase1** clock. Do this in such a way as to be independent of the absolute value of **d**, i.e. keep the timing parameterizable.

6.2 Without using a **wand** net, model a wired-AND configuration by employing open-collector NAND gates and a pullup primitive.

6.3 Model the following charge sharing circuit using appropriate trireg declarations:

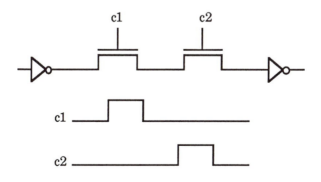

6.4 What results from passing the following strength values through a resistive MOS gate:

A) 0(00110000_00000000)

B) X(00000011_00000001)

C) 1(00000000_11111110)

6.5 In the following two examples of combining strength values, one of them has an incorrect result, which one, and what should the result be?

```
x(00000001_01111111)     output 1
0(00100000_00000000)     output 2
x(00111111_01111111)     result on net

0(01100000_00000000)     output 1
x(01111111_00111111)     output 2
0(01100000_00000000)     result on net
```

6.6 Given the following about combining strength values for a wired-AND net type:

```
0(01000000_00000000)     output 1
1(00000000_01000000)     output 2
0(01000000_00000000)     result on wired-AND net
```

What is the correct result for the following wired-AND combination?

0(01100000_00000000) output 1

1(00000000_01100000) output 2

7. Two Large Examples

7.1 THE MINISIM EXAMPLE

7.1.1 Overview

MiniSim is a description of a very simplified gate level simulator. Only three primitives have been included: a nand gate, a D positive edge-triggered flip flop, and a wire that handles the full strength algebra that is used in Verilog. All primitive timing is unit delay, and a record is kept of the stimulus pattern number and simulation time within each pattern. Each primitive is limited to two inputs and two outputs.

Two circuits are illustrated. The first to be loaded and simulated is a flip flop toggle circuit. The second circuit has two open-collector gates wired together with a pullup, and illustrates some cases when combining signal strengths.

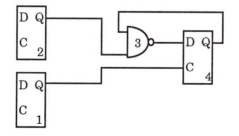

Figure 7.1. The Flip Flop Toggle Circuit.

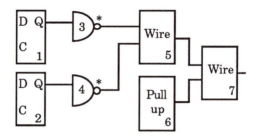

Figure 7.2. Two Open Collector Gates Driving a Wire.

7.1.2   The miniSim Source

```
module miniSim;

// element types being modeled
`define Nand 0
`define DEdgeFF 1
`define Wire 2

// literal values with strength:
//   format is 8 0-strength bits in decreasing strength order
//   followed by 8 1-strength bits in decreasing strength order
`define Strong0 16'b01000000_00000000
`define Strong1 16'b00000000_01000000
`define StrongX 16'b01111111_01111111
`define Pull0   16'b00100000_00000000
`define Pull1   16'b00000000_00100000
`define Highz0 16'b00000001_00000000
`define Highz1 16'b00000000_00000001

// three-valued logic set
`define Val0 3'd0
`define Val1 3'd1
`define ValX 3'd2

parameter //set DebugFlags to 1 for message
     DebugFlags =                     'b11000,
//                                     |||||
//   loading                       <--+||||
//   event value changes           <----+|||
//   wire calculation              <------+||
//   evaluation                    <--------+|
//   scheduling                    <----------+

     IndexSize = 16,    //maximum size for index pointers
     MaxElements = 50,  //maximum number of elements
```

```
    TypeSize = 12;      //maximum number of types

reg [IndexSize-1:0]
   eventElement,         //output value change element
   evalElement,          //element on fanout
   fo0Index[1:MaxElements], //first fanout index of eventElement
   fo1Index[1:MaxElements], //second fanout index of eventElement
   currentList,          //current time scheduled event list
   nextList,             //unit delay scheduled event list
   schedList[1:MaxElements]; //scheduled event list index
reg [TypeSize-1:0]
   eleType[1:MaxElements]; //element type
reg
   fo0TermNum[1:MaxElements],  //first fanout input terminal number
   fo1TermNum[1:MaxElements],  //second fanout input terminal number
   schedPresent[1:MaxElements]; //element is in scheduled event list flags
reg [15:0]
   eleStrength[1:MaxElements], //element strength indication
   outVal[1:MaxElements],    //element output value
   in0Val[1:MaxElements],    //element first input value
   in1Val[1:MaxElements],    //element second input value
   in0, in1, out, oldIn0;    //temporary value storage

integer pattern, simTime; //time keepers

initial
 begin
  // initialize variables
  pattern = 0;
  currentList = 0;
  nextList = 0;

  $display("Loading toggle circuit");
  loadElement(1, `DEdgeFF, 0, `Strong1,0,0, 4,0,0,0);
  loadElement(2, `DEdgeFF, 0, `Strong1,0,0, 3,0,0,0);
  loadElement(3, `Nand, (`Strong0 | `Strong1),
     `Strong0,`Strong1,`Strong1, 4,0,1,0);
  loadElement(4, `DEdgeFF, (`Strong0 | `Strong1),
     `Strong1,`Strong1,`Strong0, 3,0,1,0);

  // apply stimulus and simulate
  $display("Applying 2 clocks to input element 1");
  applyClock(2, 1);
  $display("Changing element 2 to value 0 and applying 1 clock");
  setupStim(2, `Strong0);
  applyClock(1, 1);

  $display("\nLoading open-collector and pullup circuit");
  loadElement(1, `DEdgeFF, 0, `Strong1,0,0, 3,0,0,0);
```

```
        loadElement(2, `DEdgeFF, 0, `Strong0,0,0, 4,0,0,0);
        loadElement(3, `Nand, (`Strong0 | `Highz1),
          `Strong0,`Strong1,`Strong1, 5,0,0,0);
        loadElement(4, `Nand, (`Strong0 | `Highz1),
          `Highz1,`Strong0,`Strong1, 5,0,1,0);
        loadElement(5, `Wire, 0,
          `Strong0,`Strong0,`Highz1, 7,0,1,0);
        loadElement(6, `DEdgeFF, 0, `Pull1,0,0, 7,0,0,0);
        loadElement(7, `Wire, 0,
          `Strong0,`Pull1,`Strong0, 0,0,0,0);

        // apply stimulus and simulate
        $display("Changing element 1 to value 0");
        pattern = pattern + 1;
        setupStim(1, `Strong0);
        executeEvents;
        $display("Changing element 2 to value 1");
        pattern = pattern + 1;
        setupStim(2, `Strong1);
        executeEvents;
        $display("Changing element 2 to value X");
        pattern = pattern + 1;
        setupStim(2, `StrongX);
        executeEvents;
      end

// Initialize data structure for a given element.
task loadElement;
input [IndexSize-1:0] loadAtIndex; //element index being loaded
input [TypeSize-1:0] type;       //type of element
input [15:0] strengthCoercion;    //strength specification of element
input [15:0] oVal, i0Val, i1Val; //output and input values
input [IndexSize-1:0] fo0, fo1;  //fanout element indexes
input fo0Term, fo1Term;          //fanout element input terminal indicators
  begin
    if (DebugFlags[4])
      $display(
        "Loading element %0d, type %0s, with initial value %s(%b_%b)",
        loadAtIndex, typeString(type),
        valString(oVal), oVal[15:8], oVal[7:0]);
    eleType[loadAtIndex] = type;
    eleStrength[loadAtIndex] = strengthCoercion;
    outVal[loadAtIndex] = oVal;
    in0Val[loadAtIndex] = i0Val;
    in1Val[loadAtIndex] = i1Val;
    fo0Index[loadAtIndex] = fo0;
    fo1Index[loadAtIndex] = fo1;
    fo0TermNum[loadAtIndex] = fo0Term;
    fo1TermNum[loadAtIndex] = fo1Term;
```

```
      schedPresent[loadAtIndex] = 0;
   end
 endtask

 // Given a type number, return a type string
 function [32*8:1] typeString;
 input [TypeSize-1:0] type;
    case (type)
     `Nand: typeString = "Nand";
     `DEdgeFF: typeString = "DEdgeFF";
     `Wire: typeString = "Wire";
     default: typeString = "*** Unknown element type";
    endcase
 endfunction

 // Setup a value change on an element.
 task setupStim;
 input [IndexSize-1:0] vcElement; //element index
 input [15:0] newVal;          //new element value
  begin
   if (! schedPresent[vcElement])
    begin
     schedList[vcElement] = currentList;
     currentList = vcElement;
     schedPresent[vcElement] = 1;
    end
   outVal[vcElement] = newVal;
  end
 endtask

 // Setup and simulate a given number of clock pulses to a given element.
 task applyClock;
 input [7:0] nClocks;
 input [IndexSize-1:0] vcElement;
    repeat(nClocks)
     begin
      pattern = pattern + 1;
      setupStim(vcElement, `Strong0);
      executeEvents;
      pattern = pattern + 1;
      setupStim(vcElement, `Strong1);
      executeEvents;
     end
 endtask

 // Execute all events in the current event list.
 // Then move the events in the next event list to the current event
 // list and loop back to execute these events. Continue this loop
 // until no more events to execute.
```

```
// For each event executed, evaluate the two fanout elements if present.
task executeEvents;
reg [15:0] newVal;
  begin
   simTime = 0;
   while (currentList)
    begin
     eventElement = currentList;
     currentList = schedList[eventElement];
     schedPresent[eventElement] = 0;
     newVal = outVal[eventElement];
     if (DebugFlags[3])
       $display(
         "At %0d,%0d Element %0d, type %0s, changes to %s(%b_%b)",
         pattern, simTime,
          eventElement, typeString(eleType[eventElement]),
          valString(newVal), newVal[15:8], newVal[7:0]);
     if (fo0Index[eventElement]) evalFo(0);
     if (fo1 Index[eventElement]) evalFo(1);
     if (! currentList) // if empty move to next time unit
      begin
       currentList = nextList;
       nextList = 0;
       simTime = simTime + 1;
      end
    end
  end
endtask

// Evaluate a fanout element by testing its type and calling the
// appropriate evaluation routine.
task evalFo;
input fanout; //first or second fanout indicator
  begin
   evalElement = fanout ? fo1 Index[eventElement] :
               fo0Index[eventElement];
   if (DebugFlags[1])
     $display("Evaluating Element %0d type is %0s",
        evalElement, typeString(eleType[evalElement]));
   case (eleType[evalElement])
    `Nand: evalNand(fanout);
    `DEdgeFF: evalDEdgeFF(fanout);
    `Wire: evalWire(fanout);
   endcase
  end
endtask

// Store output value of event element into
// input value of evaluation element.
```

```verilog
task storeInVal;
input fanout; //first or second fanout indicator
  begin
  // store new input value
  if (fanout ? fo1TermNum[eventElement] : fo0TermNum[eventElement])
    in1Val[evalElement] = outVal[eventElement];
  else
    in0Val[evalElement] = outVal[eventElement];
  end
endtask

// Convert a given full strength value to three-valued logic (0, 1 or X)
function [1:0] log3;
input [15:0] inVal;
  casez (inVal)
  16'b00000000_00000000: log3 = `ValX;
  16'b???????0_00000000: log3 = `Val0;
  16'b00000000_???????0: log3 = `Val1;
  default:       log3 = `ValX;
  endcase
endfunction

// Convert a given full strength value to four-valued logic (0, 1, X or Z),
// returning a 1 character string
function [8:1] valString;
input [15:0] inVal;
  case (log3(inVal))
  `Val0: valString = "0";
  `Val1: valString = "1";
  `ValX: valString = (inVal & 16'b11111110_11111110) ? "X" : "Z";
  endcase
endfunction

// Coerce a three-valued logic output value to a full output strength value
// for the scheduling of the evaluation element
function [15:0] strengthVal;
input [1:0] logVal;
  case (logVal)
  `Val0: strengthVal = eleStrength[evalElement] & 16'b11111111_00000000;
  `Val1: strengthVal = eleStrength[evalElement] & 16'b00000000_11111111;
  `ValX: strengthVal = fillBits(eleStrength[evalElement]);
  endcase
endfunction

// Given an incomplete strength value, fill the missing strength bits.
// The filling is only necessary when the value is unknown.
function [15:0] fillBits;
input [15:0] val;
  begin
```

```
    fillBits = val;
    if (log3(val) == `ValX)
      begin
        casez (val)
16'b1??????_????????: fillBits = fillBits | 16'b11111111_00000001;
16'b01??????_????????: fillBits = fillBits | 16'b01111111_00000001;
16'b001?????_????????: fillBits = fillBits | 16'b00111111_00000001;
16'b0001????_????????: fillBits = fillBits | 16'b00011111_00000001;
16'b00001???_????????: fillBits = fillBits | 16'b00001111_00000001;
16'b000001??_????????: fillBits = fillBits | 16'b00000111_00000001;
16'b0000001?_????????: fillBits = fillBits | 16'b00000011_00000001;
        endcase
        casez (val)
16'b????????_1???????: fillBits = fillBits | 16'b00000001_11111111;
16'b????????_01??????: fillBits = fillBits | 16'b00000001_01111111;
16'b????????_001?????: fillBits = fillBits | 16'b00000001_00111111;
16'b????????_0001????: fillBits = fillBits | 16'b00000001_00011111;
16'b????????_00001???: fillBits = fillBits | 16'b00000001_00001111;
16'b????????_000001??: fillBits = fillBits | 16'b00000001_00000111;
16'b????????_0000001?: fillBits = fillBits | 16'b00000001_00000011;
        endcase
      end
  end
endfunction

// Evaluate a 'Nand' gate primitive.
task evalNand;
input fanout; //first or second fanout indicator
  begin
    storeInVal(fanout);
    // calculate new output value
    in0 = log3(in0Val[evalElement]);
    in1 = log3(in1Val[evalElement]);
    out = ((in0 == `Val0) || (in1 == `Val0)) ?
      strengthVal(`Val1) :
      ((in0 == `ValX) || (in1 == `ValX)) ?
        strengthVal(`ValX):
        strengthVal(`Val0);
    // schedule if output value is different
    if (out != outVal[evalElement])
      schedule(out);
  end
endtask

// Evaluate a D positive edge-triggered flip flop
task evalDEdgeFF;
input fanout; //first or second fanout indicator
  // check value change is on clock input
  if (fanout ? (fo1TermNum[eventElement] == 0) :
```

```
              (fo0TermNum[eventElement] == 0))
        begin
          // get old clock value
          oldIn0 = log3(in0Val[evalElement]);
          storeInVal(fanout);
          in0 = log3(in0Val[evalElement]);
          // test for positive edge on clock input
          if ((oldIn0 == `Val0) && (in0 == `Val1))
           begin
             out = strengthVal(log3(in1Val[evalElement]));
             if (out != outVal[evalElement])
               schedule(out);
           end
        end
      else
         storeInVal(fanout); // store data input value
endtask

// Evaluate a wire with full strength values
task evalWire;
input fanout;
reg [7:0] mask;
 begin
   storeInVal(fanout);

   in0 = in0Val[evalElement];
   in1 = in1Val[evalElement];
   mask = getMask(in0[15:8]) & getMask(in0[7:0]) &
       getMask(in1[15:8]) & getMask(in1[7:0]);
   out = fillBits((in0 | in1) & {mask, mask});

   if (out != outVal[evalElement])
      schedule(out);

   if (DebugFlags[2])
      $display("in0 = %b_%b\nin1 = %b_%b\nmask= %b %b\nout = %b_%b",
        in0[15:8],in0[7:0], in1[15:8],in1[7:0],
        mask,mask, out[15:8],out[7:0]);
 end
endtask

// Given either a 0-strength or 1-strength half of a strength value
// return a masking pattern for use in a wire evaluation.
function [7:0] getMask;
input [7:0] halfVal; //half a full strength value
   casez (halfVal)
   8'b???????1: getMask = 8'b11111111;
   8'b??????10: getMask = 8'b11111110;
   8'b?????100: getMask = 8'b11111100;
```

```
        8'b????1000: getMask = 8'b11111000;
        8'b???10000: getMask = 8'b11110000;
        8'b??100000: getMask = 8'b11100000;
        8'b?1000000: getMask = 8'b11000000;
        8'b10000000: getMask = 8'b10000000;
        8'b00000000: getMask = 8'b11111111;
      endcase
endfunction

// Schedule the evaluation element to change to a new value.
// If the element is already scheduled then just insert the new value.
task schedule;
input [15:0] newVal; // new value to change to
  begin
    if (DebugFlags[0])
      $display(
        "Element %0d, type %0s, scheduled to change to %s(%b_%b)",
        evalElement, typeString(eleType[evalElement]),
        valString(newVal), newVal[15:8], newVal[7:0]);
    if (! schedPresent[evalElement])
      begin
        schedList[evalElement] = nextList;
        nextList = evalElement;
      end
    outVal[evalElement] = newVal;
  end
endtask
endmodule
```

7.1.3 Simulation Results

```
Loading toggle circuit
Loading element 1, type DEdgeFF, with initial value 1(01000000_00000000)
Loading element 2, type DEdgeFF, with initial value 1(01000000_00000000)
Loading element 3, type Nand, with initial value 0(00000000_01000000)
Loading element 4, type DEdgeFF, with initial value 1(01000000_00000000)
Applying 2 clocks to input element 1
At 1,0 Element 1, type DEdgeFF, changes to 0(00000000_01000000)
At 2,0 Element 1, type DEdgeFF, changes to 1(01000000_00000000)
At 2,1 Element 4, type DEdgeFF, changes to 0(00000000_01000000)
At 2,2 Element 3, type Nand, changes to 1(01000000_00000000)
At 3,0 Element 1, type DEdgeFF, changes to 0(00000000_01000000)
At 4,0 Element 1, type DEdgeFF, changes to 1(01000000_00000000)
At 4,1 Element 4, type DEdgeFF, changes to 1(01000000_00000000)
At 4,2 Element 3, type Nand, changes to 0(00000000_01000000)
Changing element 2 to value 0 and applying 1 clock
At 5,0 Element 1, type DEdgeFF, changes to 0(00000000_01000000)
At 5,0 Element 2, type DEdgeFF, changes to 0(00000000_01000000)
At 5,1 Element 3, type Nand, changes to 1(01000000_00000000)
At 6,0 Element 1, type DEdgeFF, changes to 1(01000000_00000000)
```

Loading open-collector and pullup circuit
Loading element 1, type DEdgeFF, with initial value 1(01000000_00000000)
Loading element 2, type DEdgeFF, with initial value 0(00000000_01000000)
Loading element 3, type Nand, with initial value 0(00000000_01000000)
Loading element 4, type Nand, with initial value Z(00000001_00000000)
Loading element 5, type Wire, with initial value 0(00000000_01000000)
Loading element 6, type DEdgeFF, with initial value 1(00100000_00000000)
Loading element 7, type Wire, with initial value 0(00000000_01000000)
Changing element 1 to value 0
At 7,0 Element 1, type DEdgeFF, changes to 0(00000000_01000000)
At 7,1 Element 3, type Nand, changes to Z(00000001_00000000)
At 7,2 Element 5, type Wire, changes to Z(00000001_00000000)
At 7,3 Element 7, type Wire, changes to 1(00100000_00000000)
Changing element 2 to value 1
At 8,0 Element 2, type DEdgeFF, changes to 1(01000000_00000000)
At 8,1 Element 4, type Nand, changes to 0(00000000_01000000)
At 8,2 Element 5, type Wire, changes to 0(00000000_01000000)
At 8,3 Element 7, type Wire, changes to 0(00000000_01000000)
Changing element 2 to value X
At 9,0 Element 2, type DEdgeFF, changes to X(01111111_01111111)
At 9,1 Element 4, type Nand, changes to X(00000001_01111111)
At 9,2 Element 5, type Wire, changes to X(00000001_01111111)
At 9,3 Element 7, type Wire, changes to X(00111111_01111111)

7.2   THE 8251A EXAMPLE

7.2.1   Overview

The following example is a description of the Intel 8251A device, which is a serial communication receiver and transmitter. The description contains examples of synchronous and asynchronous concurrent activities, explicit timing checks, error handling, and diagnostics. Cadence Design Systems, Inc. does not guarantee the accuracy or completeness of this model. Anyone using this does so at their own risk. Intel and MCS are trademarks of the Intel Corporation.

7.2.2   The 8251A Source

```
/*
DEVICE INFO
  CHIP NAME: 8251A
  MFGR: Intel
  DESCRIPTION: Programmable communication interface (USART)
    TYPE:
    SIZE:
    FUNCTIONAL NAME: USART
        (Universal Synchronous/Asynchronous Receiver/Transmitter)
  TECHNOLOGY: N-channel silicon gate
FILE INFO:
  THIS FILE: 8251A.v
  FILES USED:
  USED BY FL:
  DOC FILES:  8251A.doc
  TEST FILES: 8251A_stimulus.t 8251A_tests.t test[1-15].t
DESIGN INFO
  DESIGNER: Chi-Lai Huang / Tom Meyer
  DSN DATE: 8/25/87
  MODIFICN: None
    BY:
  REFERENCES: Intel MCS-80 data book
TEST INFO
  TESTED BY: Tom Meyer
  TEST DATE: 9/10/87
VERIFY INFO
  VERIFIED BY: Sanjay Nayak
  VERIFY  DATE: 9/20/87
*/


// Parity check means the number of 1's in data and parity bit should be
// even for even parity, odd for odd parity.
```

```
module I8251A(dbus,rcd,gnd,txc_,write_,chipsel_,comdat_,read_,rxrdy,
       txrdy,syndet,cts_,txe,txd,clk,reset,dsr_,rts_,dtr_,rxc_,vcc);

parameter [7:0] instance_id = 8'h00;

   parameter [8:1] dflags      =       8'b00000100;
   //                                            |||||
   // diagnostic dflags:                         |||||
   // bit 5 (16)  operation event trace  <-+||||
   // bit 4 (8)   communication errors   <---+|||
   // bit 3 (4)   timing check           <-----+||
   // bit 2 (2) = print receiving        <-------+|
   // bit 1 (1) = print transmitting <---------+
```

/* timing constants, for A. C. timing check, only non-zero times
   are specified, in nano-sec */

/* read cycle */
`define TRR 250
`define TRD 200
`define TDF 100 // max. time used

/* write cycle */
`define TWW 250
`define TDW 150
`define TWD 20
`define TRV 6 // in terms of clock cycles

/* other timing */
`define TTXRDY 8 // 8 clock cycles

input
    rcd, // receive data
    rxc_, // receive clock
    txc_, // transmit clock
    chipsel_, // chip selected when low
    comdat_, // command/data_ select
    read_, write_,
    dsr_, // data set ready
    cts_, // clear to send
    reset,// reset when high
    clk, // at least 30 times of the transmit/receive data bit rates
    gnd,
    vcc;

output
    rxrdy, // receive data ready when high
    txd, // transmit data line
    txrdy, // transmit buffer ready to accept another byte to transfer

```
    txe, // transmit buffer empty
    rts_, // request to send
    dtr_; // data terminal ready

inout[7:0]
    dbus;

inout
    syndet; //outside synchonous detect or output to indicate syn det

supply0
    gnd;
supply1
    vcc;

reg
    txd,
    rxrdy,
    txe,
    dtr_,
    rts_;

reg[7:0]
    receivebuf,
    rdata,
    status;

reg
    recvdrv,
    statusdrv;

assign
    // if recvdrv 1 dbus is driven by rdata
    dbus = recvdrv ? rdata : 8'bz,
    dbus = statusdrv ? status : 8'bz;

reg[7:0]
    command,
    tdata_out, // data being transmitted serially
    tdata_hold, // data to be transmitted next if tdata_out is full
    sync1, sync2, // synchronous data bytes
    modreg;
and  (txrdy,status[0],command[0], ~ cts_);

reg transmitter_reset, // set to 1 upon a reset, cleared upon write data
    tdata_out_full, // 1 if data in tdata_out has not been transmitted.
    tdata_hold_full, // 1 if data in tdata_hold has not been transferred to
             //  tdata_out for serial transmission.
    tdata_hold_cts; // 1 if tdata_hold_full and it was cts when data was
```

```
                       //  transferred to tdata_hold.
                       // 0 if tdata_hold is empty or is full but was filled
                       //  while it was not cts.

    reg tdata_out_wait; // 0 if a stop bit was just sent and we do not need
                        //  to wait for a negedge on txc before transmitting

    reg[7:0] syncmask;
    nmos  syndet_gate1(syndet,status[6], ~ modreg[6]);

    reg   sync_to_receive; // 1(2) if looking for 1st(2nd) sync on rxd
    reg   syncs_received; // 1 if sync chars received, 0 if looking for sync(s)
    reg   rec_sync_index; // indicating the syn. character to be matched

    integer  breakcount_period; // number of clock periods to count as break

    reg   sync_to_transmit;  // 1(2) if 1st(2nd) sync char should be sent next

    reg[7:0] data_mask;   // masks off the data bits (if char size is not 8)
    // temporary registers
    reg[1:0] csel;         // indicates what next write means if comdat_=1:
                           // (0=mode instruction,1=sync1,2=sync2,3=command)
    reg[5:0]
      baudmx,
      tbaudcnt,
      rbaudcnt; // baud rate
    reg[7:0]
      tstoptotal; // no. of tranmit clock pulses for stop bit (0 if sync mode)
    reg[3:0]
      databits;   // no. of data bits in a character (5,6,7 or 8)

    reg
      rdatain; // a data byte is read in if 1

    reg was_cts_when_received;  // 0: if cts_ was high when char was received
                    // 1: if cts_ was low when char was received
                    //  (and so char was sent before shutdown)

    event
      resete,
      start_receiver_e;

    reg receive_in_progress;


    event txende;
```

```
                /*** COMMUNICATION ERRORS ***/

task frame_error;
  begin
    if(dflags[4])
      $display("I8251A (%h) at %d: *** frame error",
                            instance_id, $time);
    status[5]=1;
  end
endtask

task parity_error;
  begin
    if(dflags[4])
      $display("I8251A (%h) at %d: *** parity error on data: %b",
                      instance_id, $time, receivebuf);
    status[3]=1;
  end
endtask

task overrun_error;
  begin
    if(dflags[4])
      $display("I8251A (%h) at %d: *** overrun error",
                            instance_id, $time);
    status[4]=1;
  end
endtask



                /*** TIMING VIOLATIONS ***/

integer
  time_dbus_setup,
  time_write_begin,
  time_write_end,
  time_read_begin,
  time_read_end,
  between_write_clks; // to check between write recovery
reg reset_signal_in;   // to check the reset signal pulse width

initial
begin
  time_dbus_setup  = -9999;
  time_write_begin = -9999;
  time_write_end   = -9999;
  time_read_begin  = -9999;
  time_read_end    = -9999;
```

```
     between_write_clks = `TRV; // start: TRV clk periods since last write

end



     /** Timing analysis for read cycles **/

always @(negedge read_)
  if (chipsel_==0)
  begin
    time_read_begin=$time;
    read_address_watch;
  end

  /* Timing violation: read pulse must be TRR ns */

always @(posedge read_)
  if (chipsel_==0)
  begin
    disable read_address_watch;
    time_read_end=$time;

    if(dflags[3] && (($time-time_read_begin) < `TRR))
      $display("I8251A (%h) at %d: *** read pulse width violation",
                         instance_id, $time);
  end

  /* Timing violation: address (comdat_ and chipsel_) must be stable */
  /*              stable throughout read                 */

task read_address_watch;
  @(comdat_ or chipsel_) // if the "address" changes
    if (read_==0)      //   and read_ did not change at the same time
      if (dflags[3])
        $display("I8251A (%h) at %d: *** address hold error on read",
                         instance_id, $time);
endtask

     /** Timing analysis for write cycles **/

always @(negedge write_)
  if (chipsel_==0)
  begin
    time_write_begin=$time;
    write_address_watch;
  end
```

```
    /* Timing violation: read pulse must be TRR ns */
    /* Timing violation: TDW ns bus setup time before posedge write_ */
    /* Timing violation: TWD ns bus hold  time after  posedge write_ */

always @(posedge write_)
  if(chipsel_==0)
  begin
    disable write_address_watch;
    time_write_end=$time;

    if(dflags[3] && (($time-time_write_begin) < `TWW))
      $display("I8251A (%h) at %d: *** write pulse width violation",
                            instance_id, $time);

    if(dflags[3] && (($time-time_dbus_setup) < `TDW))
      $display("I8251A (%h) at %d: *** data setup violation on write",
                            instance_id, $time);
  end

always @dbus
  begin
    time_dbus_setup=$time;

    if(dflags[3] && (($time-time_write_end < `TWD)))
      $display("I8251A (%h) at %d: *** data hold violation on write",
                            instance_id, $time);
  end


    /* Timing violation: address (comdat_ and chipsel_) must be stable */
    /*            stable throughout write            */

task write_address_watch;
   @(comdat_ or chipsel_) // if the "address" changes
     if(write_==0)    //   and write_ did not change at the same time
       if(dflags[3])
         $display("I8251A (%h) at %d: *** address hold error on write",
                            instance_id, $time);
endtask


    /* Timing violation: minimum of TRV clk cycles between writes */

always @(negedge write_)
  if(chipsel_== 0)
  begin
    time_write_begin=$time;
    if(dflags[3] && between_write_clks < `TRV)
      $display("I8251A (%h) at %d: *** between write recovery violation",
```

```
                                    instance_id, $time);
       between_write_clks = 0;
    end

  always @(negedge write_)
    repeat (`TRV) @(posedge clk)
      between_write_clks = between_write_clks + 1;



       /** Timing analysis for reset sequence **/

    /* Timing violation: reset pulse must be 6 clk cycles */

  always @(posedge reset)
    begin :reset_block
    reset_signal_in=1;
    repeat(6) @(posedge clk);
    reset_signal_in=0;
    // external reset
    -> resete;
    end

  always @(negedge reset)
    begin
    if(dflags[3] && (reset_signal_in==1))
       $display("I8251A (%h) at %d: *** reset pulse too short",
                                 instance_id, $time);
    disable reset_block;
    end



       /*** BEHAVIORAL DESCRIPTION ***/


    /* Reset sequence */

initial
    begin // power-on reset
    reset_signal_in=0;
    ->resete;
    end

  always @resete
    begin
    if(dflags[5])
       $display("I8251A (%h) at %d: performing reset sequence",
```

```
                              instance_id, $time);
        csel=0;
        transmitter_reset=1;
        tdata_out_full=0;
        tdata_out_wait=0;
        tdata_hold_full=0;
        tdata_hold_cts=0;
        rdatain=0;
        status=4; // only txe is set
        txe=1;
        statusdrv=0;
        recvdrv=0;
        txd=1; // line at mark state upon reset until data is transmitted
        // assign not allowed for status, etc.
        rxrdy=0;
        command=0;
        dtr_=1;
        rts_=1;
        status[6]=0; // syndet is reset to output low
        sync_to_transmit=1;    // transmit sync char #1 when sync are transmt'd
        sync_to_receive=1;
        between_write_clks = `TRV;
        receive_in_progress=0;
        disable read_address_watch;
        disable write_address_watch;
        disable trans1;
        disable trans2;
        disable trans3;
        disable trans4;
        disable rcv_blk;
        disable sync_hunt_blk;
        disable double_sync_hunt_blk;
        disable parity_sync_hunt_blk;
        disable syn_receive_internal;
        disable asyn_receive;
        disable break_detect_blk;
        disable break_delay_blk;
      end


  always @(negedge read_)
    if (chipsel_==0)
    begin
      #(`TRD) // time for data to show on the data bus

      if (comdat_==0)    // 8251A DATA ==> DATA BUS
      begin
        recvdrv=1;
        rdatain=0; // no receive byte is ready
```

```
          rxrdy=0;
          status[1]=0;
       end
       else              // 8251A STATUS ==> DATA BUS
       begin
          statusdrv=1;
          if (modreg [1:0] == 2'b00) // if sync mode
             status[6]=0;         //   reset syndet upon status read
                         // Note: is only reset upon reset
                         //     or rxd=1 in async mode
       end
    end

  always @(posedge read_)
    begin
       #(`TDF) // data from read stays on the bus after posedge read_
       recvdrv=0;
       statusdrv=0;
    end


  always @(negedge write_)
  begin
    if((chipsel_==0) && (comdat_==0))
    begin
      txe=0;
       status[2]=0; // transmitter not empty after receiving data
       status[0]=0; // transmitter not ready after receiving data
    end
  end


  always @(posedge write_)         // read the command/data from the CPU
    if (chipsel_==0)
    begin
      if (comdat_==0)      // DATA BUS ==> 8251A DATA
      begin
        case (command[0] & ~ cts_)
        0:                // if it is not clear to send
        begin
          tdata_hold=dbus;
           tdata_hold_full=1;//   then mark the data as received and
           tdata_hold_cts=0; //   that it should be sent when cts
        end
        1:                // if it is clear to send ...
         if(transmitter_reset) // ... and this is 1st data since reset
         begin
           transmitter_reset=0;
           tdata_out=dbus;
```

```
        tdata_out_wait=1; //   then wait for a negedge on txc
        tdata_out_full=1; //        and transmit the data
        tdata_hold_full=0;
        tdata_hold_cts=0;
         repeat(`TTXRDY) @(posedge clk);
        status[0]=1;    //        and set the txrdy status bit
    end
     else              // ... and a sync/data char is being sent
     begin
        tdata_hold=dbus; //   then mark the data as being received
        tdata_hold_full=1;//   and that it should be transmitted if
        tdata_hold_cts=1; //   it becomes not cts,
                    //   but do not set the txrdy status bit
    end
    endcase
end
else              // DATA BUS ==> CONTROL
begin
    case (csel)
    0:              // case 0:  MODE INSTRUCTION
    begin
        modreg=dbus;
        if(modreg[1:0]==0)   // synchronous mode
        begin
         csel=1;
         baudmx=1;
          tstoptotal=0; // no stop bit for synch. op.
        end
        else
         begin              // asynchronous mode
          csel=3;
           baudmx=1; // 1X baud rate
           if(modreg[1:0]==2'b10)baudmx=16;
           if(modreg[1:0]==2'b11)baudmx=64;
           // set up the stop bits in clocks
           tstoptotal=baudmx;
           if(modreg[7:6]==2'b10)tstoptotal=
                tstoptotal+baudmx/2;
           if(modreg[7:6]==2'b11)tstoptotal=
                tstoptotal+tstoptotal;
        end
         databits=modreg[3:2]+5; // bits per char
         data_mask=255 >> (3-modreg[3:2]);
    end

    1:          // case 1:  1st SYNC CHAR - SYNC MODE
    begin
        sync1=dbus;
         /* the syn. character will be adjusted to the most
```

```
          significant bit to simplify syn. hunt,
          syncmask is also set to test the top data bits  */
       case (modreg[3:2])
     0:
      begin
        sync1=sync1 << 3;
        syncmask=8'b11111000;
      end

      1:
      begin
        sync1=sync1 << 2;
        syncmask=8'b11111100;
      end

      2:
      begin
        sync1=sync1 << 1;
        syncmask=8'b11111110;
      end
      3:
          syncmask=8'b11111111;
       endcase

      if(modreg[7]==0)
          csel=2;  // if in double sync char mode, get 2 syncs
      else
          csel=3;  // if in single sync char mode, get 1 sync
    end

    2:          // case 2: 2nd SYNC CHAR - SYNC MODE
    begin
       sync2=dbus;
       case (modreg[3:2])
       0: sync2=sync2 << 3;
       1: sync2=sync2 << 2;
       2: sync2=sync2 << 1;
       endcase

      csel=3;
    end

    3:   // case 3:  COMMAND INSTRUCTION - SYNC/ASYNC MODE
    begin
       status[0]=0; // Trick: force delay txrdy pin if command[0]=1
       command=dbus;
       dtr_= ! command[1];

       if(command[3])          // if send break command
```

```
            assign txd=0;      //   set txd=0 (ignores/overrides
          else                 //   later non-assign assignments)
            deassign txd;

          if(command[4]) status[5:3]=0; // Clear Frame/Parity/Overrun
          rts_= ! command[5];
          if(command[6]) ->resete;    // internal reset

          if(modreg[1:0]==0 && command[7])
          begin                // if sync mode and enter hunt
            disable            //   disable the sync receiver
              syn_receive_internal;
            disable
              syn_receive_external;

            receivebuf=8'hff;  //   reset recieve buffer 1's
            -> start_receiver_e; //   restart sync mode receiver
          end

          if(receive_in_progress==0)
            -> start_receiver_e;

          repeat(`TTXRDY) @(posedge clk);
          status[0]=1;
        end
      endcase
    end
  end


reg [7:0] serial_data;
reg parity_bit;


always wait (tdata_out_full==1)
begin :trans1

  if(dflags[1])
    $display("I8251A (%h) at %d: transmitting data: %b",
            instance_id, $time, tdata_out);

  if (tdata_out_wait)              // if the data arrived any old time
    @(negedge txc_);               //   wait for a negedge on txc_
                      // but if a stop bit was just sent
                      //   do not wait
  serial_data=tdata_out;

  if (tstoptotal != 0)             // if async mode ...
  begin
```

```
   txd=0;                    //  then send a start bit 1st
     repeat(baudmx) @(negedge txc_);
   end

   repeat(databits)              // send all start, data bits
   begin
     txd=serial_data[0];
      repeat(baudmx) @(negedge txc_);
      serial_data=serial_data>> 1;
   end

   if (modreg [4])                // if parity is enabled ...
   begin
     parity_bit= ^ (tdata_out & data_mask);
     if(modreg[5]==0)parity_bit= ~parity_bit; // odd parity

     txd=parity_bit;
      repeat(baudmx) @(negedge txc_); //   then send the parity bit
   end

   if(tstoptotal != 0)            // if sync mode
   begin
     txd=1;                 //   then send out the stop bit(s)
     repeat(tstoptotal) @(negedge txc_);
   end

    tdata_out_full=0;// block this routine until data/sync char to be sent
             // is immediately transferred to tdata_out.

    ->txende;      // decide what data should be sent (data/sync/stop bit)
   end

event transmit_held_data_e,
    transmitter_idle_e;

always @txende               // end of transmitted data/sync character
begin :trans2

   case (command[0] & ~ cts_)
   0:                 // if it is not now cts
                  // but data was received while it was cts
    if (tdata_hold_full && tdata_hold_cts)
      -> transmit_held_data_e; // then send the data char
   else
      -> transmitter_idle_e;  // else send sync char(s) or 1 stop bit

   1:                 // if it is now cts
    if (tdata_hold_full)      // if a character has been received
                  //    but not yet transmitted ...
```

```
      -> transmit_held_data_e; //      then send the data char

  else                 //   else (no character has been received)
     -> transmitter_idle_e; //      send sync char(s) or 1 stop bit
  endcase
end


always @transmitter_idle_e    // if there are no data chars to send ...
begin :trans3
  status[2]=1;           //      mark transmitter as being empty
  txe=1;


  if (tstoptotal != 0 | |   //      if async mode or after a reset
    command[0]==0 | | cts_==1)//       or TxEnable=false or cts_=false
  begin
    if(dflags[1])
       $display("I8251A (%h) at %d: transmitting data: 1 (stop bit)",
                              instance_id, $time);

    txd=1;            //      then send out 1 stop bit
    tdata_out=1;          //             and make any writes
                //             go to tdata_hold
    repeat(baudmx) @(negedge txc_);
    -> txende;
  end
  else              //      if sync mode
   case (sync_to_transmit)
   1:                //      ... send 1st sync char now
     begin
     tdata_out=sync1 >> (8-databits);
     tdata_out_wait=0;   //        without waiting on negedge txc
     tdata_out_full=1;
     if(modreg[7]==0)    //      if double sync mode
        sync_to_transmit=2;//       send 2nd sync after 1st
     end
   2:                //      ... send 2nd sync char now
     begin
     tdata_out=sync2 >> (8-databits);
     tdata_out_wait=0;   //        without waiting on negedge txc
     tdata_out_full=1;
     sync_to_transmit=1;  //      send 1st sync char next
     end
   endcase
end


always @ transmit_held_data_e //   if a character has been received
```

```
begin :trans4
  tdata_out=tdata_hold;     //      but not transmitted ...
  tdata_out_wait=0;         //      then do not wait on negedge txc
  tdata_out_full=1;         //         and send the char immediately
  tdata_hold_full=0;
  repeat(`TTXRDY) @(posedge clk);
  status[0]=1;              //      and set the txrdy status bit
end


/************ RECEIVER PORTION OF THE 8251A ************/

              // data is received at leading edge of the clock

event break_detect_e,  //
    break_delay_e;     //

event hunt_sync1_e,      // hunt for the 1st sync char
    hunt_sync2_e,        // hunt for the 2nd sync char (double sync mode)
    sync_hunted_e,       // sync char(s) was found (on a bit aligned basis)
    external_syndet_watche;// external sync mode: whenever syndet pin
              // goes high, set the syndet status bit


always @start_receiver_e
begin :rcv_blk
  receive_in_progress=1;

  case(modreg[1:0])
  2'b00:
    if(modreg[6]==0)            // if internal syndet mode ...
    begin
      if(dflags[5])
        $display("I8251A (%h) at %d: starting internal sync receiver",
                        instance_id, $time);

      if(dflags[5] && command[7])
        $display("I8251A (%h) at %d: hunting for syncs",
                        instance_id, $time);

      if(modreg[7]==1)      //  if enter hunt mode
      begin
        if(dflags[5])
          $display("I8251A (%h) at %d: receiver waiting on syndet",
                        instance_id, $time);

        -> hunt_sync1_e;     //   start search for sync char(s)
                  //   & wait for syncs to be found
        @(posedge syndet);
```

```
            if(dflags[5])
                $display("I8251A (%h) at %d: receiver DONE waiting on syndet",
                                instance_id, $time);
        end

            syn_receive_internal;    // start sync mode receiver
        end
        else                    // if external syndet mode ...
        begin
          if(dflags[5])
              $display("I8251A (%h) at %d: starting external sync receiver",
                                instance_id, $time);

          if(dflags[5] && command[7])
              $display("I8251A (%h) at %d: hunting for syncs",
                                instance_id, $time);

          -> external_syndet_watche;//   whenever syndet pin goes to 1
                          //      set syndet status bit

          if (command[7]==1)      //   if enter hunt mode
          begin :external_syn_hunt_blk
          fork
              syn_receive_external;//      assemble chars while waiting

              @(posedge syndet)  //       after rising edge of syndet
                @(negedge syndet) //       wait for falling edge
                      //      before starting char assembly
                  disable external_syn_hunt_blk;
            join
          end

          syn_receive_external;       // start external sync mode receiver
        end

      default:                // if async mode ...
        begin
          if(dflags[5])
              $display("I8251A (%h) at %d: starting asynchronous receiver",
                                instance_id, $time);

            -> break_detect_e;     //    start check for rcd=0 too long
            asyn_receive;          //    and start async mode receiver
        end
      endcase
    end
```

```
             /**** EXTERNAL SYNCHRONOUS MODE RECEIVE ****/

task syn_receive_external;
forever
begin
  repeat(databits)  // Whether in hunt mode or not, assemble a character
  begin
    @(posedge rxc_)
    receivebuf={rcd, receivebuf[7:1]};
  end

  get_and_check_parity;   // reveive and check parity bit, if any

  mark_char_received;     // set rxrdy line, if enabled
end
endtask

always @external_syndet_watche
  @(posedge rxc_)
    status[6]=1;

        /**** INTERNAL SYNCHRONOUS MODE RECEIVE ****/


    /* Hunt for the sync char(s)              */
    /* (if in synchronous internal sync detect mode) */
    /* Syndet is set high when the sync(s) are found */

always @ hunt_sync1_e    // search for 1st sync char in the data stream
begin :sync_hunt_blk
  while(!(((receivebuf ^ sync1) & syncmask)===8'b00000000))
  begin
    @(posedge rxc_)
    receivebuf={rcd, receivebuf[7:1]};
  end
  if(modreg[7]==0)    // if double sync mode
    -> hunt_sync2_e;  //   check for 2nd sync char directly after 1st
  else
    -> sync_hunted_e; // if single sync mode, sync hunt is complete
end

always @ hunt_sync2_e // find the second synchronous character
begin :double_sync_hunt_blk
  repeat(databits)
  begin
    @(posedge rxc_)
    receivebuf={rcd, receivebuf[7:1]};
  end
  if(((receivebuf ^ sync2) & syncmask)===8'b00000000)
```

```verilog
        ->sync_hunted_e;  // if sync2 followed syn1, sync hunt is complete
    else
        ->hunt_sync1_e;   // else hunt for sync1 again

    // Note: the data stream [sync1 sync1 sync2] will have sync detected.
    // Suppose sync1=11001100:
    // then [1100 1100 1100 sync2] will NOT be detected.
    // In general: never let a suffix of sync1 also be a prefix of sync1.
end

always @ sync_hunted_e
begin :parity_sync_hunt_blk
    get_and_check_parity;
    status[6]=1;          // set syndet status bit (sync chars detected)
end

task syn_receive_internal;
forever
begin
    repeat(databits)  // no longer in hunt mode so read entire chars and
    begin             // then look for syncs (instead of on bit boundaries)
        @(posedge rxc_)
        receivebuf={rcd, receivebuf[7:1]};
    end


    case (sync_to_receive)
    2:                          // if looking for 2nd sync char ...
    begin
        if(((receivebuf ^ sync2)
                & syncmask)===0)
        begin                   // ... and 2nd sync char is found
            sync_to_receive=1;  //   then look for 1st sync (or data)
            status[6]=1;        //      and mark sync detected
        end
        else if(((receivebuf ^ sync1)
                & syncmask)===0)
        begin                   // ... and 1st sync char is found
            sync_to_receive=2;  //   then look for 2nd sync char
        end
    end
    1:                          // but if looking for 1st or data ...
    begin
        if(((receivebuf ^ sync1)    // ... and 1st sync is found
                & syncmask)===0)
        begin
            if(modreg[7]==0)    //   if double sync mode
                sync_to_receive=2;  //    look for 2nd sync to follow
            else                //    else look for 1st or data
```

```
          status[6]=1;        //        and mark sync detected
      end
      else ;              // ... and data was found, do nothing
    end
    endcase

    get_and_check_parity;   // reveive and check parity bit, if any

    mark_char_received;
end
endtask



task get_and_check_parity;
begin
   receivebuf=receivebuf >> (8-databits);
   if (modreg[4]==1)
   begin
      @(posedge rxc_)
      if((^receivebuf ^ modreg[5] ^ rcd) != 1)
         parity_error;
   end
end
endtask



task mark_char_received;
begin
   if (command[2]==1)     // if receiving is enabled
   begin
      rxrdy=1;
      status[1]=1;       //   set receive ready status bit
      if (rdatain==1)    //   if previous data was not read
         overrun_error;  //      overrun error

      rdata=receivebuf;  //   latch the data
      rdatain=1;         //   mark data as not having been read
   end

   if(dflags[2])
      $display("I8251A (%h) at %d: received data: %b",
                     instance_id, $time, receivebuf);
end
endtask


     /********** ASYNCHRONOUS MODE RECEIVER **********/
```

```
    /* Check for break detection (rcd low through 2 */
    /* receive sequences) in the asynchronous mode. */

always @ break_detect_e
begin :break_detect_blk
  #1 /* to be sure break_delay_blk is waiting on break_deley_e
      after it triggered break_detect_e */

  if(rcd==0)
  begin
    -> break_delay_e;//start + databits + parity   + stop bit
    breakcount_period =  1   + databits + modreg[4] + (tstoptotal != 0);

        // the number of rxc periods needed for 2 receive sequences
    breakcount_period = 2 * breakcount_period * baudmx;

            // If rcd stays low through 2 consecutive
            // (start,data,parity,stop) sequences ...
    repeat(breakcount_period)
      @(posedge rxc_);
    status[6]=1;       // ... then set break detect (status[6]) high
  end
end

always @break_delay_e
begin : break_delay_blk
  @(posedge rcd)        // but if rcd goes high during that time ...
  begin :break_delay_blk
    disable break_detect_blk;
    status[6]=0;      // ... then set the break detect low
    @(negedge rcd)     //    and when rcd goes low again ...
    -> break_detect_e;  //    ... start the break detection again
  end
end


        /**** ASYNCHRONOUS MODE RECEIVE TASK ****/

task asyn_receive;
forever
  @(negedge rcd) // the receive line went to zero, maybe a start bit
  begin
    rbaudcnt = baudmx / 2;
    if(baudmx==1)
      rbaudcnt=1;
    repeat(rbaudcnt) @(posedge rxc_); // after half a bit ...
```

```
        if (rcd == 0)              // if it is still a start bit
        begin
          rbaudcnt=baudmx;
          repeat(databits)          //   receive the data bits
          begin
             repeat(rbaudcnt) @(posedge rxc_);
             #1 receivebuf= {rcd, receivebuf[7:1]};
          end

          repeat(rbaudcnt) @(posedge rxc_);


          // shift the data to the low part
          receivebuf=receivebuf >> (8-databits);

          if (modreg[4]==1)         // if parity is enabled
          begin
             if((^receivebuf ^ modreg[5] ^ rcd) != 1)
                parity_error;        //   check for a parity error

             repeat(rbaudcnt) @(posedge rxc_);
          end

          #1 if (rcd==0)            // if middle of stop bit is 0
             frame_error;           //   frame error (should be 1)

          mark_char_received;
      end
    end
  endtask
endmodule
```

7.3 EXERCISES

7.1 Extend the miniSim description to include a NAND latch element as specified in Example 1.10.

7.2 Extend the miniSim description to include a bufif1 gate element. What output values are generated when the control input is unknown and the data input is 0 or 1?

7.3 Add another net type that models a two input wired-AND element to the miniSim description. This element must allow the 0-strength component to win in situations of equal 0 and 1 strength (hint: the solution involves an alteration of the masking operation only).

Appendix A. Lexical Conventions

Verilog source text files consist of a stream of lexical tokens separated by white space. The spacing of tokens is free format -- the specific choice of tabs, spaces, or newlines to separate lexical tokens is not important to the compiler. However, the choice is important for giving a readable structure to the description. It is important that you develop a consistent style of writing your Verilog descriptions. We offer the examples in the book as a starting point to develop your own personal style.

The types of lexical tokens in the language are: white space, comments, operators, numbers, strings, identifiers, and keywords. This Appendix will discuss each of these.

A.1 WHITE SPACE AND COMMENTS

White space is defined as any of the following characters: blanks, tabs, newlines, and formfeeds. These are ignored except for when they are found in strings.

There are two forms of comments. The single line comment begins with the two characters // and ends with a newline. A block comment begins with the two characters /* and ends with the two characters */. Block comments may span several lines. However, they may not be nested.

A.2 OPERATORS

Operators are single, double or triple character sequences that are used in expressions. Appendix B lists and defines all the operators.

A.3 NUMBERS

Constant numbers can be specified in decimal, hexadecimal, octal, or binary. They may optionally start with a + or -, and can be given in one of two forms.

The first form is an unsized decimal number specified using the digits from the sequence 0 to 9. Although the designer may not specify the size, Verilog calculates a size for use in an expression. In an expression, the size is typically equivalent to the size of the operator's other (sized) operand. The appropriate number of bits, starting from the least significant bit, are selected for use. Appendix B lists a set of rules for calculating the size.

The second form specifies the size of the constant and takes the form:

ss . . s 'f nn . . n

where:

ss . . s   is the size in bits of the constant. The size is specified as a decimal number.

'f   is the base format. The **f** is replaced by one of the single letters: d, h, o, or b, for decimal, hexadecimal, octal, or binary. The letters may also be capitalized.

nn . . n   is the value of the constant specified in the given base with allowable digits. For the hexadecimal base, the letters **a** through **f** may also be capitalized.

Unknown and high impedance values may be given in all but the decimal base. In each case, the **x** or **z** character represents the given number of bits of **x** or **z**. i.e. in hexadecimal, an **x** would represent four unknown bits, in octal, three.

Normally, zeros are padded on the left if the number of bits specified in **nn . . n** is less than specified by **ss . . s**. However, if the first digit of **nn . . n** is **x** or **z**, then **x** or **z** is padded on the left.

An underline character may be inserted into a number (of any base) to improve readability. It must not be the first character of a number. For instance, the binary number:

        12 'b 0x0x_1101_0zx1

is more readable than:

        12 'b 0x0x11010zx1.

Examples of unsized constants are:

        792   // a decimal number

        7d9   // illegal, hexadecimal must be specified with 'h

        'h 7d9   // an unsized hexadecimal number

        'o 7746   // an unsized octal number

Examples of sized constants are:

        12 'h x   // a 12 bit unknown number

        8 'h fz   // equivalent to the binary: 8 'b 1111_zzzz

        10 'd 17   // a ten bit constant with the value 17.

A.4 STRINGS

A string is a sequence of characters enclosed by double quotes. It must be contained on a single line. Special characters may be specified in a string using the "\" escape character as follows:

        \n   new line character. Typically the **return** key.

        \t   tab character. Equivalent to typing the tab key.

        \\   is the \ character.

        \"   is the " character

        \ddd   is an ASCII character specified in one to three octal digits.

A.5 IDENTIFIERS, SYSTEM NAMES, AND KEYWORDS

Identifiers are names that are given to elements such as modules, registers, wires, instances, and begin-end blocks. An identifier is any sequence of letters, digits, and the underscore (_) symbol except that:

- the first character must not be a digit, and

- the identifier must be 1024 characters or less.

Upper and lower case letters are considered to be different.

System tasks and functions are identifiers that always start with the dollar ($) symbol. A partial list of system tasks and functions is provided in Appendix E.

Escaped identifiers allow for any printable ASCII character to be included in the name. Escaped identifiers begin with white space. The backslash ("\") character leads off the identifier, which is then terminated with white space. The leading backslash character is not considered part of the identifier.

Examples of escaped identifiers include:

```
\bus-index
\a+b
```

Escaped identifiers are used for translators from other CAD systems. These systems may allow special characters in identifiers. Escaped identifiers should not be used under normal circumstances.escaped identifier

Verilog keywords are listed below:

always	endspecify	negedge	rtranif0	wait
and	endtable	nmos	rtranif1	wand
assign	endtask	nor	scalered	weak0
begin	event	not	small	weak1
buf	for	notif0	specify	while
bufif0	force	notif1	specparam	wire
bufif1	forever	or	strong0	wor
case	fork	output	strong1	xnor
casex	function	pmos	supply0	xor
casez	highz0	posedge	supply1	
cmos	highz1	primitive	table	
deassign	if	pull0	task	
default	initial	pull1	time	
defparam	inout	pulldown	tran	
disable	input	pullup	tranif0	
edge	integer	rcmos	tranif1	
else	join	reg	tri	
end	large	release	tri0	
endcase	macromodule	repeat	tri1	
endfunction	medium	rnmos	triand	
endmodule	module	rpmos	trior	
endprimitive	nand	rtran	vectored	

Appendix B. Verilog Operators

B.1 TABLE OF OPERATORS

Operator Symbol	Name	Definition	Comments
{ , }	Concatenation	Joins together bits from two or more comma-separated expressions	Constants must be sized. Alternate form uses a repetition multiplier. {b, {3 {a, b}}} is equivalent to {b, a, b, a, b, a, b}.
+	Addition	Sums two operands.	Register and net operands are treated as unsigned. Real and integer operands may be signed. If any bit is unknown, the result will be unknown.
-	Subtraction	Finds difference between two operands.	Register and net operands are treated as unsigned. Real and integer operands may be signed. If any bit is unknown, the result will be unknown.
-	Unary minus	Changes the sign of its operand	Register and net operands are treated as unsigned. Real and integer operands may be signed. If any bit is unknown, the result will be unknown.

*	Multiplication	Multiply two operands.	Register and net operands are treated as unsigned. Real and integer operands may be signed. If any bit is unknown, the result will be unknown.
/	Division	Divide two operands	Register and net operands are treated as unsigned. Real and integer operands may be signed. If any bit is unknown, the result will be unknown. Divide by zero produces an **x**.
%	Modulus	Find remainder	Register and net operands are treated as unsigned. Real and integer operands may be signed. If any bit is unknown, the result will be unknown.
>	Greater than	Determines relative value	Register and net operands are treated as unsigned. Real and integer operands may be signed. If any bit is unknown, the relation is ambiguous and the result will be unknown.
>=	Greater than or equal	Determines relative value	Register and net operands are treated as unsigned. Real and integer operands may be signed. If any bit is unknown, the relation is ambiguous and the result will be unknown.
<	Less than	Determines relative value	Register and net operands are treated as unsigned. Real and integer operands may be signed. If any bit is unknown, the relation is ambiguous and the result will be unknown.
<=	Less than or equal	Determines relative value	Register and net operands are treated as unsigned. Real and integer operands may be signed. If any bit is unknown, the relation is ambiguous and the result will be unknown.

!	Logical negation	Unary Complement	Converts a non-zero value (TRUE) into zero; a zero value (FALSE) into one; and an ambiguous truth value into **x**.
&&	Logical AND	ANDs two logical values.	Used as a logical connective in, for instance, **if** statements. e.g. if ((a > b) && (c < d)).
||	Logical OR	ORs two logical values.	Used as a logical connective in, for instance, **if** statements. e.g. if ((a > b) || (c < d)).
==	Logical equality	Compares two values for equality	Register and net operands are treated as unsigned. Real and integer operands may be signed. If any bit is unknown, the relation is ambiguous and the result will be unknown.
==	Logical inequality	Compares two values for inequality	Register and net operands are treated as unsigned. Real and integer operands may be signed. If any bit is unknown, the relation is ambiguous and the result will be unknown.
===	Case equality	Compares two values for equality	The bitwise comparison includes comparison of **x** and **z** values. All bits must match for equality. The result is either TRUE or FALSE.
!==	Case inequality	Compares two values for inequality	The bitwise comparison includes comparison of **x** and **z** values. Any bit difference produces inequality. The result is either TRUE or FALSE.
~	Bitwise negation	Complements each bit in the operand	Each bit of the operand is complemented. The complement of **x** is **x**.
&	Bitwise AND	Produces the bitwise AND of two operands.	See truth table below

	Bitwise OR	Produces the bitwise inclusive OR of two operands.	See truth table below
^	Bitwise XOR	Produces the bitwise exclusive OR of two operands.	See truth table below
^~ or ~^	Equivalence	Produces the bitwise exclusive NOR of two operands	See truth table below
&	Unary reduction AND	Produces the single bit AND of all of the bits of the operand.	Unary reduction and binary bitwise operators are distinguished by syntax.
~&	Unary reduction NAND	Produces the single bit NAND of all of the bits of the operand.	Unary reduction and binary bitwise operators are distinguished by syntax.
		Unary reduction OR	Produces the single bit inclusive OR of all of the bits of the operand.	Unary reduction and binary bitwise operators are distinguished by syntax.
~|	Unary reduction NOR	Produces the single bit NOR of all of the bits of the operand.	Unary reduction and binary bitwise operators are distinguished by syntax.
^	Unary reduction XOR	Produces the single bit XOR of all of the bits of the operand.	Unary reduction and binary bitwise operators are distinguished by syntax.

~^ or ^~	Unary reduction XNOR	Produces the single bit XNOR of all of the bits of the operand.	Unary reduction and binary bitwise operators are distinguished by syntax.
<<	Left shift	Shift the left operand left by the number of bit positions specified by the right operand	Vacated bit positions are filled with zeros
>>	Right shift	Shift the left operand right by the number of bit positions specified by the right operand	Vacated bit positions are filled with zeros
?:	Conditional	Assign one of two values based on expression	condExpr ? trueExpr : falseExpr. If condExpr is TRUE, the trueExpr is the result of the operator. If condExpr is FALSE, the falseExpr is the result. If the condExpr is ambiguous, then both trueExpr and falseExpr expressions are calculated and the result is produced in a bitwise fashion. For each bit, if both expression bits are one, the result is one. If both are zero, the result is zero. Otherwise, the resulting bit is **x**.

B.2   OPERATOR PRECEDENCE

The operator precedences are shown below. The top of the table is the highest precedence, and the bottom is the lowest. Operators listed on the same line have the same precedence. All operators associate left to right in an expression. Parentheses can be used to change the precedence or clarify the situation. When in doubt, use parentheses. They are easier to read, and reread!

unary operators: ! & ~& | ~| ^ ~^ + -   (highest precedence)

$$* \ / \ \%$$

$$+ \ -$$

$$<< \ >>$$

$$< \ <= \ > \ >=$$

$$== \ != \ === \ !==$$

$$\& \ ^\wedge \ \sim^\wedge$$

$$|$$

$$\&\&$$

$$||$$

?:   (lowest precedence)

B.3   OPERATOR TRUTH TABLES

B.3.1   Bitwise AND

&	0	1	x
0	0	0	0
1	0	1	x
x	0	x	x

B.3.2 Bitwise OR

$\mid$	0	1	x
0	0	1	x
1	1	1	1
x	x	1	x

B.3.3 Bitwise XOR

$\wedge$	0	1	x
0	0	1	x
1	1	0	x
x	x	x	x

B.3.4 Bitwise XNOR

$\sim\wedge$	0	1	x
0	1	0	x
1	0	1	x
x	x	x	x

B.4 EXPRESSION BIT LENGTHS

In the following table, $L(i)$ refers to the length in bits of operand i.

Expression	Bit Length	Comments
unsized constant number	same as integer (usually 32)	
sized constant number	as given	
i OP j	max $(L(i), L(j))$	OP is +, -, /, *, %, &, |, ^, ~^
+i, -i	$L(i)$	
~i	$L(i)$	
i OP j	1 bit	OP is ===, !==, ==, !=, &&, ||, <, <=, >, >= and the reduction operators &, ~&, |, ~|, ^, ~^
i >> j, i << j	$L(i)$	
i ? j : k	max $(L(j), L(k))$	
{i, ..., j}	$L(i) + ... + L(j)$	
{i {j, ..., k}}	$i * (L(j) + ... + L(k))$	

Appendix C. Verilog Gate Types

C.1 LOGIC GATES

These gates all have one scaler output and any number of scaler inputs. When instantiating one of these modules, the first parameter is the output and the rest are inputs. Zero, one or two delays may be specified for the propagation times. Strengths may be specified on the outputs.

AND	0	1	x	z
0	0	0	0	0
1	0	1	x	x
x	0	x	x	x
z	0	x	x	x

NAND	0	1	x	z
0	1	1	1	1
1	1	0	x	x
x	1	x	x	x
z	1	x	x	x

OR	0	1	x	z
0	0	1	x	x
1	1	1	1	1
x	x	1	x	x
z	x	1	x	x

NOR	0	1	x	z
0	1	0	x	x
1	0	0	0	0
x	x	0	x	x
z	x	0	x	x

XOR	0	1	x	z
0	0	1	x	x
1	1	0	x	x
x	x	x	x	x
z	x	x	x	x

XNOR	0	1	x	z
0	1	0	x	x
1	0	1	x	x
x	x	x	x	x
z	x	x	x	x

C.2 BUF AND NOT GATES

These gates have one or more scaler outputs and one scaler input. The input is listed last on instantiation. Zero, one, or two delays may be specified. Strengths may be specified on the outputs.

BUF	output
0	0
1	1
x	x
z	x

NOT	output
0	1
1	0
x	x
z	x

C.3 BUFIF AND NOTIF GATES

These gates model three-state drivers. Zero, one, two, or three delays may be specified. Each of the gates has one output, one data input, and one control input. On instantiation, the ports are listed in that order. (L indicates 0 or z; H indicates 1 or z)

		Control Input			
	Bufif0	0	1	x	z
D	0	0	z	L	L
A	1	1	z	H	H
T	x	x	z	x	x
A	z	x	z	x	x

		Control Input			
	Bufif1	0	1	x	z
D	0	z	0	L	L
A	1	z	1	H	H
T	x	z	x	x	x
A	z	z	x	x	x

		Control Input			
	Notif0	0	1	x	z
D	0	1	z	H	H
A	1	0	z	L	L
T	x	x	z	x	x
A	z	x	z	x	x

	Notif1	Control Input			
		0	1	x	z
D	0	z	1	H	H
A	1	z	0	L	L
T	x	z	x	x	x
A	z	z	x	x	x

C.4 MOS GATES

These gates model NMOS and PMOS transistors. The "r" versions model NMOS and PMOS transistors with significantly higher resistivity when conducting. The resistive forms reduce the driving strength from input to output. The nonresistive forms only reduce the supply strength to a strong strength. See Table 6.7. Drive strengths may not be specified for these gates.

Each gate has one scaler output, one scaler data input, and one scaler control input, and on instantiation, are listed in that order. (L indicates 0 or z; H indicates 1 or z)

	(r)pmos	Control Input			
		0	1	x	z
D	0	0	z	L	L
A	1	1	z	H	H
T	x	x	z	x	x
A	z	z	z	z	z

		Control Input			
	(r)nmos	0	1	x	z
D	0	z	0	L	L
A	1	z	1	H	H
T	x	z	x	x	x
A	z	z	z	z	z

C.5　BIDIRECTIONAL GATES

The following gates are true bidirectional transmission gates: tran, tranif1, tranif0, rtran, rtranif1, and rtranif0. Each of these has two scaler inout terminals. The tranif and rtranif gates have a control input which is listed last on instantiation.

The rise delay indicates the turn-on delay for the pass device and the fall delay indicates the turn-off delay.

C.6　CMOS GATES

CMOS gates represent the typical situation where nmos and pmos transistors are paired together to form a transmission gate. The first terminal is the data output, the second is the data input, the third is the n-channel control, and the last is the p-channel control. The cmos gate is a relatively low impedance device. The rcmos version has a higher impedance when conducting.

C.7　PULLUP AND PULLDOWN GATES

These are single output gates that drive pull strength values (the default) onto the output net. Pullup drives a logic one and pulldown drives a logic zero. The strength may be specified.

Appendix D. Registers, Memories, Integers, and Time

D.1 REGISTERS

Registers are abstractions of storage devices found in digital systems. They are defined with the **reg** keyword and are optionally given a size (or bit width). The default size is one. Thus:

        reg   tempBit;

defines a single bit register named **tempBit**, while

        reg   [15:0] tempNum;

defines a 16-bit register named tempNum. Single bit registers are termed *scaler*, and multiple bit registers are termed *vector*. The bit width specification gives the name of the most significant bit first (in this case, 15) and the least significant bit last. The register could have been declared as

        reg   [0:15] tempNum;

with the only difference being that the most significant bit is named (numbered) 0. Of course, all the other bits are differently numbered.

Either a single bit, or several contiguous bits of a vector register (or net) can be addressed and used in an expression. Selecting a single bit is called a *bit select*, and selecting several contiguous bits is known as a *part select*. Examples of these include:

```
reg   [10:0]   counter;
reg            a;
reg   [2:0]    b;
...
a = counter[7];        // bit seven of counter is loaded into a
b = counter[4:2];      // bits 4, 3, 2 of counter are loaded into b
```

In a bit select, the bit to be selected may be specified with an expression or by a literal. The bits selected in a part select must be specified with constant expressions or literals.

D.2 MEMORIES

Memories are defined using the register declaration:

```
reg    [10:0]  lookUpTable [0:31];
```

This declares a 32 word array named **lookUpTable** where each word consists of 11 bits. The memory is used in an expression, for example, as follows:

```
lookUpTable [5] = 75;
```

This would load the fifth word of **lookUpTable** with the value 75.

Bit selects and part selects are not allowed with memories. To specify this, the memory must be first transferred to a register and then a bit or part select may be performed on the register.

D.3 INTEGERS AND TIMES

Registers are used to model hardware. Sometimes though, it is useful to perform calculations for simulation purposes. For example, we may want to turn off monitoring after a certain time has passed. If we use registers for this purpose, the operations on them may be confused with actions of the actual hardware. *Integer* and *time* variables provide a means of describing calculations pertinent to the simulation. They are provided for convenience and make the description more self documenting.

An integer declaration uses the *integer* keyword and specifies a list of variables. The time declaration is the same except for the *time* keyword:

```
integer  a, b;          //two integers
integer  c [1:100];     // an array of integers
time     q, r;          // two time variables
time     s [1:100];     // an array of times
```

An integer is a general purpose 32-bit variable. Operations on it are assumed to be two's complement and the most significant bit indicates the sign.

A time variable is a 64-bit variable typically used with the $time system function.

Appendix E. System Tasks and Functions

In this section we present some of the built in Verilog System Tasks and Functions. Our philosophy for this book is not to become a substitute for the simulator manual. Rather, we want to illustrate a few of the basic methods of displaying the results of simulation, and stopping the simulation.

E.1 DISPLAY AND WRITE TASKS

There are two main tasks for printing information during a simulation: $display and $write. These two are the same except that $display always prints a newline character at the end of its execution. Examples of the $display task were given throughout the main portion of the book. A few details will be given here.

The typical form of the parameters to these tasks is

$display ("Some text %d and maybe some more: %h.", a, b);

This statement would print the quoted string with the value of **a** substituted in for the format control "%d", and **b** is substituted in for the format control "%h". The "%d" indicates that the value should be printed in a decimal base. %h specifies hexadecimal.

Allowable letters in the format control specification are:

h or H   display in hexadecimal
d or D   display in decimal
o or O   display in octal
b or B   display in binary
c or C   display ASCII character
v or V   display net signal strength (see "printed abbreviation" in Table 6.4.
m or M   display hierarchical name
s or S   display string

Using the construct "%0d" will print a decimal number without leading zeros or spaces. This may be used with **h**, **d**, and **o** also.

Two adjacent commas (,,) will print a single space. Other special characters may be printed with escape sequences:

\n   is the new line character
\t   is the tab character
\\   is the \ character
\"   is the " character
\ddd   is the character specified in up to 3 octal digits

For instance:

$display ("Hello world\n");

will print the quoted string with two newline characters (remember, $display automatically adds one at the end of its execution).

E.2 CONTINUOUS MONITORING

The $monitor command is used to print information whenever there is a *change* in one or more specified values. The monitor prints at the end of the current time so that all changes at the current time will be reflected by the printout. The parameters for the $monitor task are the same as for the $display task.

The command is:

$monitor (parameters as used in the $display task);

Whenever the $monitor task is called, it will print the values and set up the simulator to print them anytime one of the parameters changes. Only one $monitor display list may be active at a time. If time is being printed as in the following $monitor statement, a change in simulation time will not trigger the $monitor to print.

$monitor ($time,, "regA = ", regA);

E.3 STROBED MONITORING

The $strobe task also uses the same parameter list format as the $display task. Unlike $display, it will print just before simulation time is about to advance. In this way, $strobe insures that all of the changes that were made at the current simulation time have been made, and thus will be printed.

E.4 FILE OUTPUT

The $display, $write, $monitor, and $strobe tasks have a version for writing to a file. They each require an extra parameter, called the file descriptor, as shown below:

$fdisplay (descriptor, parameters as in the display command);
$fwrite (descriptor, parameters as in the write command);
$fmonitor (descriptor, parameters as in the monitor command);
$fstrobe (descriptor, parameters as in the strobe command);

The descriptor is a 32-bit value returned from the $fopen function. The descriptor may be stored in a 32-bit reg. The $fopen function takes the form:

$fopen ("name of file");

$fopen will return 0 if it was unable to open the file for writing. When finished writing to a file, it is closed with the function call:

$fclose (descriptor);

The descriptors are set up so that each bit of the descriptor indicates a different channel. Thus, multiple calls to $fopen will return a different bit set. The least significant bit indicates the "standard output" (typically a terminal) and need not be opened. By passing the OR of two or more descriptors to one of the printing commands, the same message will be printed into all of the files (and standard output) indicated by the ORed descriptors.

E.5 SIMULATION TIME

$time is a function that returns the current time as a 64-bit value. $stime will return a 32-bit value. The time may be printed, for instance, with the $monitor command as shown below:

```
$monitor ($time,,, "regA = ", regA);
```

Note that the change of simulation time will not trigger the $monitor to print.

E.6 STOP AND FINISH

The $stop and $finish tasks stop simulation. They differ in that $stop returns control back to the simulator's command interpreter, while $finish returns back to the host operating system.

```
$stop;
$stop(n);
$finish;
$finish(n);
```

A parameter may be passed to these tasks with the following effects.

Parameter Value	Diagnostics
0	prints nothing
1	gives simulation time and location
2	same as 1, plus a few lines of run statistics

If the forms with no parameter are used, then the default is the same as passing a 1 to it.

E.7 RANDOM

The $random system function provides a random number mechanism, returning a new random number each time the function is called. The size of the returned value is the same as an integer variable. The function may be called with or without a parameter:

```
$random;
$random(<seed>);
```

The <seed> parameter is an inout which is used to control the numbers that $random returns. An argument for <seed> must be a register, integer, or time variable, and should be assigned to the variable before calling $random.

Appendix F. Formal Syntax Definition

The following items summarize the format of the formal syntax descriptions:

1. White space may be used to separate lexical tokens

2. Angle brackets surround each description item and are not literal symbols. That is, they do not appear in the source description. Any text outside angle brackets is literal.

3. <name> in lower case is a syntax construct item.

4. <NAME> in upper case is a lexical token item. Its definition is a terminal node in the description hierarchy-that is, its definition does not contain any syntax construct items.

5. <name>? is an optional item

6. <name>* is zero, one or more items

7. <name>+ is one or more items

8. <name> <,<name>>* is a comma separated list of items with at least one item in the list

9. <name> ::= gives a syntax definition to an item

10. | |= introduces an alternative syntax definition

The syntax description of the Verilog language follows this rule: every item referenced in one section is completely defined in that section, or an item cross-references the section that finishes its definition.

F.1 SOURCE TEXT

<source_text>
      ::= <description>*

<description>
      ::= <module>
      | | = <primitive>

<module>
      ::= module <name_of_module> <list_of_ports>? ;
          <module_item>*
          endmodule
      | | = macromodule <name_of_module> <list_of_ports>? ;
          <module_item>*
          endmodule

<name_of_module>
      ::= <IDENTIFIER>   Defined in Section F.8.

<list_of_ports>
      ::= (<port> <,<port>>*)

<port>
      ::= <port_expression>?
      | | = . <name_of_port> (<port_expression>?)

<port_expression>
      ::= <port_reference>
      | | = { <port_reference> <,<port_reference>>* }

<port_reference>
      ::= <name_of_variable>
      | | = <name_of_variable> [<constant_expression>]
      | | = <name_of_variable> [<constant_expression> :
          <constant_expression>]

<name_of_port>
      ::= <IDENTIFIER>

<name_of_variable>
    ::= <IDENTIFIER>

<module_item>
    ::= <parameter_declaration>   Defined in Section F.2.
    | | = <input_declaration>   Defined in Section F.2.
    | | = <output_declaration>   Defined in Section F.2.
    | | = <inout_declaration>   Defined in Section F.2.
    | | = <net_declaration>   Defined in Section F.2.
    | | = <reg_declaration>   Defined in Section F.2.
    | | = <time_declaration>   Defined in Section F.2.
    | | = <integer_declaration>   Defined in Section F.2.
    | | = <real_declaration>   Defined in Section F.2.
    | | = <event_declaration>   Defined in Section F.2.
    | | = <gate_instantiation>   Defined in Section F.3.
    | | = <primitive_instantiation> .   Defined in Section F.3.
    | | = <module_instantiation>   Defined in Section F.4.
    | | = <parameter_override>   Defined in Section F.2.
    | | = <continuous_assign>   Defined in Section F.2.
    | | = <specify_block>   Defined in Section F.6.
    | | = <initial_statement>   Defined in Section F.5.
    | | = <always_statement>   Defined in Section F.5.
    | | = <task>
    | | = <function>

<primitive>
    ::= primitive <name_of_primitive> (<name_of_variable>
       <,<name_of_variable>>*) ;
    <prim_declaration>+
    <table_definition>
    endprimitive

<name_of_primitive>
    ::= <IDENTIFIER>

<prim_declaration>
    ::= <output_declaration>   Defined in Section F.2.
    | | = <reg_declaration>   Defined in Section F.2.
    | | = <input_declaration>   Defined in Section F.2.

<table_definition>
    ::= table <table_entries> endtable

<table_entries>

```
    ::= <combinational_entry>+
    | | = <sequential_entry>+
```

<combinational_entry>
```
    ::= <level_input_list> : <OUTPUT_SYMBOL> ;
```

<sequential_entry>
```
    ::= <input_list> : <state> : <next_state> ;
```

<input_list>
```
    ::= <level_input_list>
    | | = <edge_input_list>
```

<level_input_list>
```
    ::= <LEVEL_SYMBOL>+
```

<edge_input_list>
```
    ::= <LEVEL_SYMBOL>* <edge> <LEVEL_SYMBOL>*
```

<edge>
```
    ::= ( <LEVEL_SYMBOL> <LEVEL_SYMBOL> )
    | | = <EDGE_SYMBOL>
```

<state>
```
    ::= <LEVEL_SYMBOL>
```

<next_state>
```
    ::= <OUTPUT_SYMBOL>
    | | = - (This is a literal hyphen, see Chapter 5 for details)
```

<OUTPUT_SYMBOL> is one of the following characters:
```
    0 1 x X
```

<LEVEL_SYMBOL> is one of the following characters:
```
    0 1 x X ? b B
```

<EDGE_SYMBOL> is one of the following characters:
```
    r R f F p P n N *
```

<task>
```
    ::= task <name_of_task> ;
        <tf_declaration>*<statement_or_null> endtask
```

<name_of_task>
```
    ::= <IDENTIFIER>
```

<function>
       ::= function <range_or_type>? <name_of_function> ;
       <tf_declaration>+
       <statement_or_null>   Defined in Section F.5.
       endfunction

<range_or_type>
       ::= <range>   Defined in Section F.2.
       | |= integer
       | |= real

<name_of_function>
       ::= <IDENTIFIER>

<tf_declaration>
       ::= <parameter_declaration>   Defined in Section F.2.
       | |= <input_declaration>   Defined in Section F.2.
       | |= <output_declaration>   Defined in Section F.2.
       | |= <inout_declaration>   Defined in Section F.2.
       | |= <reg_declaration>   Defined in Section F.2.
       | |= <time_declaration>   Defined in Section F.2.
       | |= <integer_declaration>   Defined in Section F.2.
       | |= <real_declaration>   Defined in Section F.2.
       | |= <event_declaration>   Defined in Section F.2.

F.2 DECLARATIONS

<parameter_declaration>
       ::= parameter <list_of_assignments> ;

<input_declaration>
       ::= input <range>? <list_of_variables> ;

<output_declaration>
       ::= output <range>? <list_of_variables> ;

<inout_declaration>
       ::= inout <range>? <list_of_variables> ;

<net_declaration>
       ::= <NETTYPE> <expandrange>? <delay>?
           <list_of_variables> ;
       | |= trireg <charge_strength>? <expandrange>? <delay>?
           <list_of_variables> ;

```
    | | = <NETTYPE> <drive_strength>? <expandrange>? <delay>?
        <list_of_assignments> ;
```

<NETTYPE> is one of the following keywords:
    wire tri tri1 supply0 wand triand tri0 supply1 wor trior

<expandrange>
```
    ::= <range>
    | | = scalared <range>
    | | = vectored <range>
```

<delay>   Defined in Section F.8.

<reg_declaration>
```
    ::= reg <range>? <list_of_register_variables> ;
```

<time_declaration>
```
    ::= time <list_of_register_variables> ;
```

<integer_declaration>
```
    ::= integer <list_of_register_variables> ;
```

<real_declaration>
```
    ::= real <list_of_variables> ;
```

<event_declaration>
```
    ::= event <name_of_event> <,<name_of_event>>* ;
```

<continuous_assign>
```
    ::= assign <drive_strength>? <delay>? <list_of_assignments> ;
```

<parameter_override>
```
    ::= defparam <list_of_assignments> ;
```

<list_of_variables>
```
    ::= <name_of_variable> <,<name_of_variable>>*
```

<list_of_register_variables>
```
    ::= <register_variable> <,<register_variable>>*
```

<register_variable>
```
    ::= <name_of_register>
    | | = <name_of_memory> [ <constant_expression> :
        <constant_expression> ]
```

<constant_expression>   Defined in Section F.7.

<name_of_register>
  ::= <IDENTIFIER>   Defined in Section F.8.

<name_of_memory>
  ::= <IDENTIFIER>   Defined in Section F.8.

<name_of_event>
  ::= <IDENTIFIER>   Defined in Section F.8.

<charge_strength>
  ::= (small)
  | | = (medium)
  | | = (large)

<drive_strength>
  ::= (<STRENGTH0> , <STRENGTH1>)
  | | = (<STRENGTH1> , <STRENGTH0>)

<STRENGTH0> is one of the following keywords:
  supply0 strong0 pull0 weak0 highz0

<STRENGTH1> is one of the following keywords:
  supply1 strong1 pull1 weak1 highz1

<range>
  ::= [<constant_expression> <: <constant_expression>>?]

<list_of_assignments>
  ::= <assignment> <,<assignment>>*

<expression>   Defined in Section F.7.

<assignment>   Defined in Section F.5.

F.3 PRIMITIVE INSTANCES

<gate_instantiation>
  ::= <GATETYPE> <drive_strength>? <delay>?
   <gate_instance>
  <,<gate_instance>>* ;

<GATETYPE> is one of the following keywords:

and nand or nor xor xnor buf bufif0 bufif1 not notif0 notif1
pulldown pullup nmos rnmos pmos rpmos cmos rcmos tran rtran
tranif0 rtranif0 tranif1 rtranif1

<drive_strength>   Defined in Section F.2.

<delay>   Defined in Section F.8.

<gate_instance>
    ::= <name_of_gate_instance>? (<terminal> <,<terminal>>*)

<name_of_gate_instance>
    ::= <IDENTIFIER>   Defined in Section F.8.

<primitive_instantiation>
    ::= <name_of_primitive> <drive_strength>? <delay>?
        <primitive_instance> <,<primitive_instance>>* ;

<name_of_primitive>
    ::= <IDENTIFIER>   Defined in Section F.8.

<primitive_instance>
    ::= <name_of_primitive_instance>? (<terminal>
        <,<terminal>>*)

<name_of_primitive_instance>
    ::= <IDENTIFIER>   Defined in Section F.8.

<terminal>
    ::= <expression>   Defined in Section F.7.

F.4 MODULE INSTANTIATIONS

<module_instantiation>
    ::= <name_of_module> <parameter_value_assignment>?
        <module_instance> <,<module_instance>>* ;

<name_of_module>
    ::= <IDENTIFIER>   Defined in Section F.8.

<parameter_value_assignment>
    ::= # (<expression> <,<expression>>*)

<module_instance>
    ::= <name_of_instance> (<list_of_module_connections>?)

<name_of_instance>
        ::= <IDENTIFIER>   Defined in Section F.8.

<list_of_module_connections>
        ::= <module_port_connection> <,<module_port_connection>>*
        | | = <named_port_connection> <,<named_port_connection>>*

<module_port_connection>
        ::= <expression>   Defined in Section F.7.
        | | = <NULL>

<NULL>
        ::= nothing-this form covers the case of an empty item in a list, for
            example:
            (a, b, , d)

<named_port_connection>
        ::= .< IDENTIFIER> (<expression>)

<expression>   Defined in Section F.7.

F.5 BEHAVIORAL STATEMENTS

<initial_statement>
        ::= initial <statement>

<always_statement>
        ::= always <statement>

<statement_or_null>
        ::= <statement>
        | | = ;

<statement>
        ::= <assignment> ;
        | | = if (<expression>) <statement_or_null>
        | | = if (<expression>) <statement_or_null> else
            <statement_or_null>
        | | = case (<expression>) <case_item>+ endcase
        | | = casez (<expression>) <case_item>+ endcase
        | | = casex (<expression>) <case_item>+ endcase
        | | = forever <statement>
        | | = repeat (<expression>) <statement>
        | | = while (<expression>) <statement>

```
| |= for ( <assignment> ; <expression> ; <assignment> )
    <statement>
| |= <delay_control> <statement_or_null>
```
                                        Defined in Section F.8.
```
| |= <event_control> <statement_or_null>
```
                                        Defined in Section F.8.
```
| |= <lvalue> = <delay_control> <expression> ;
| |= <lvalue> = <event_control> <expression> ;
| |= wait ( <expression> ) <statement_or_null>
| |= -> <name_of_event> ;
| |= <seq_block>
| |= <par_block>
| |= <task_enable>
| |= <system_task_enable>
| |= disable <name_of_task> ;
| |= disable <name_of_block> ;
| |= assign <assignment> ;
| |= deassign <lvalue> ;
```

<assignment>
```
::= <lvalue> = <expression>
```

<lvalue>   Defined in Section F.7.

<expression>   Defined in Section F.7.

<case_item>
```
::= <expression> <,<expression>>* : <statement_or_null>
| |= default : <statement_or_null>
| |= default <statement_or_null>
```

<seq_block>
```
::= begin <statement>* end
| |= begin : <name_of_block> <block_declaration>*
    <statement>* end
```

<par_block>
```
::= fork <statement>* join
| |= fork : <name_of_block> <block_declaration>*
    <statement>* join
```

<name_of_block>
```
::= <IDENTIFIER>
```

<block_declaration>

```
    ::= <parameter_declaration>          Defined in Section F.2.
    | | = <reg_declaration>              Defined in Section F.2.
    | | = <integer_declaration>          Defined in Section F.2.
    | | = <real_declaration>             Defined in Section F.2.
    | | = <time_declaration>             Defined in Section F.2.
    | | = <event_declaration>            Defined in Section F.2.
```

<task_enable>
```
    ::= <name_of_task> ;                 Defined in Section F.1.
    | | = <name_of_task> ( <expression> <,<expression>>* ) ;
```

<system_task_enable>
```
    ::= <name_of_system_task> ;
    | | = <name_of_system_task> ( <expression> <,<expression>>* )
       ;
```

<name_of_system_task>
```
    ::= <SYSTEM_IDENTIFIER>              Defined in Section F.7.
```

F.6 SPECIFY SECTION

<specify_block>
```
    ::= specify <specify_item>* endspecify
```

<specify_item>
```
    ::= <specparam_declaration>
    | | = <path_declaration>
    | | = <level_sensitive_path_declaration>
    | | = <edge_sensitive_path_declaration>
    | | = <system_timing_check>
```

<specparam_declaration>
```
    ::= specparam <list_of_assignments> ;
```

<path_declaration>
```
    ::= <path_description> = <path_delay_value> ;
```

<path_description>
```
    ::= ( <specify_input_terminal_descriptor> =>
        <specify_output_terminal_descriptor> )
    | | = ( <list_of_path_inputs> *> <list_of_path_outputs> )
```

<list_of_path_inputs>
```
    ::= <specify_input_terminal_descriptor>
        <,<specify_input_terminal_descriptor>>*
```

\<list_of_path_outputs\>
       ::= \<specify_output_terminal_descriptor\>
          \<,\<specify_output_terminal_descriptor\>\>*

\<specify_input_terminal_descriptor\>
       ::= \<input_identifier\>
       | | = \<input_identifier\> [\<constant_expression\>]
       | | = \<input_identifier\> [\<constant_expression\> :
          \<constant_expression\>]

\<specify_output_terminal_descriptor\>
       ::= \<output_identifier\>
       | | = \<output_identifier\> [\<constant_expression\>]
       | | = \<output_identifier\> [\<constant_expression\> :
          \<constant_expression\>]

\<input_identifier\>
       ::= the \<IDENTIFIER\> of a module input or inout terminal

\<output_identifier\>
       ::= the \<IDENTIFIER\> of a module output or inout terminal

\<path_delay_value\>
       ::= \<path_delay_expression\>
       | | = (\<path_delay_expression\>, \<path_delay_expression\>)
       | | = (\<path_delay_expression\>, \<path_delay_expression\>,
          \<path_delay_expression\>)
       | | = (\<path_delay_expression\>, \<path_delay_expression\>,
          \<path_delay_expression\>, \<path_delay_expression\>,
          \<path_delay_expression\>, \<path_delay_expression\>)

\<path_delay_expression\>
       ::= \<expression\>

\<system_timing_check\>
       ::= $setup (\<timing_check_event\>, \<timing_check_event\>,
          \<timing_check_limit\>   \<,\<notify_register\>\>?) ;
       | | = $hold (\<timing_check_event\>, \<timing_check_event\>,
          \<timing_check_limit\>   \<,\<notify_register\>\>?) ;
       | | = $period (\<controlled_timing_check_event\>,
          \<timing_check_limit\>   \<,\<notify_register\>\>?) ;
       | | = $width (\<controlled_timing_check_event\>,
          \<timing_check_limit\> \<,\<constant_expression\>,
          \<notify_register\>\>?) ;

```
        | |= $skew ( <timing_check_event>, <timing_check_event>,
          <timing_check_limit> <,<notify_register>>? ) ;
        | |= $recovery ( <controlled_timing_check_event>,
          <timing_check_event>, <timing_check_limit>
          <,<notify_register>>? ) ;
        | |= $setuphold ( <timing_check_event>, <timing_check_event>,
          <timing_check_limit>, <timing_check_limit>
          <,<notify_register>>? ) ;
```

<timing_check_event>
```
    ::=  <timing_check_event_control>?
         <specify_terminal_descriptor>    <&&&
         <timing_check_condition>>?
```

<specify_terminal_descriptor>
```
    ::=  <specify_input_terminal_descriptor>
    | |=<specify_output_terminal_descriptor>
```

<controlled_timing_check_event>
```
    ::=  <timing_check_event_control>
         <specify_terminal_descriptor> <&&&
         <timing_check_condition>>?
```

<timing_check_event_control>
```
    ::= posedge
    | |= negedge
```

<timing_check_condition>
```
    ::=  <SCALAR_EXPRESSION>
    | |= ~<SCALAR_EXPRESSION>
    | |= <SCALAR_EXPRESSION> == <scalar_constant>
    | |= <SCALAR_EXPRESSION> === <scalar_constant>
    | |= <SCALAR_EXPRESSION> != <scalar_constant>
    | |= <SCALAR_EXPRESSION> !== <scalar_constant>
```

<SCALAR_EXPRESSION> is a one bit net or a bit select of an expanded vector net.

<timing_check_limit>
```
    ::=  <constant_expression>            Defined in Section F.7.
```

<scalar_constant>
```
    ::= 1'b0
    | |= 1'b1
    | |= 1'B0
```

```
| | = 1'B1
```

<notify_register>
```
::=  <identifier>
```

<level_sensitive_path_declaration>
```
::= if (<conditional_port_expression>)
    (<specify_terminal_descriptor> <polarity_operator>?=>
    <specify_terminal_descriptor>) = <path_delay_value>
| | = if (<conditional_port_expression>)  (<list_of_path_inputs>
    <polarity_operator>? *>    <list_of_path_outputs>) =
    <path_delay_value>
NOTE:  The following two symbols are literal symbols, not
    syntax description conventions:
        *>
        =>
```

<conditional_port_expression>
```
::= <port_reference>
| | = <UNARY_OPERATOR><port_reference>
| | = <port_reference><BINARY_OPERATOR><port_reference>
```

<polarity_operator>
```
::= +
| | = -
```

<edge_sensitive_path_declaration>
```
::=<if (<expression>)>?
   (<edge_identifier>?<specify_terminal_descriptor>=>
   (<specify_terminal_descriptor> <polarity_operator> ?:
   <expression>)) = <path_delay_value>
| | =<if (<expression>)>?
   (<edge_identifier>?<specify_terminal_descriptor> *>
   (<list_of_path_outputs> <polarity_operator> ?:
   <expression>)) = <path_delay_value>
```

<edge_identifier>
```
::= posedge
| | = negedge
```

F.7 EXPRESSIONS

<lvalue>
```
::= <identifier>                    Defined in Section F.8.
| | = <identifier> [ <expression> ]
```

```
| | = <identifier> [ <constant_expression> :
    <constant_expression> ]
| | = <concatenation>
```

<constant_expression>
```
::=<expression>
```

<mintypmax_expression>
```
::= <expression>
| | = <expression> : <expression> : <expression>
```

<expression>
```
::= <primary>
| | = <UNARY_OPERATOR> <primary>
| | = <expression> <BINARY_OPERATOR> <expression>
| | = <expression> <QUESTION_MARK> <expression> :
    <expression>
| | = <STRING>
```

<UNARY_OPERATOR> is one of the following tokens:
```
+ - ! ~ & ~& | ^| ^ ~^
```

<BINARY_OPERATOR> is one of the following tokens:
```
+ - * / % == != === !== && || < <= > >= & | ^ ^~ >> <<
```

<QUESTION_MARK> is ? (a literal question mark)

<STRING> is text enclosed in '" and contained on one line

<primary>
```
::= <number>
| | = <identifier>                    Defined in Section F.8.
| | = <identifier> [ <expression> ]
| | = <identifier> [ <constant_expression> :
    <constant_expression> ]
| | = <concatenation>
| | = <multiple_concatenation>
| | = <function_call>
| | = ( <mintypmax_expression> )
```

<number>
```
::= <DECIMAL_NUMBER>
| | = <UNSIGNED_NUMBER>? <BASE> <NUMBER>
| | = <REAL_NUMBER>
```

<DECIMAL_NUMBER>
::= A number containing a set of any of the following characters,
optionally preceded by + or -
0123456789_

<UNSIGNED_NUMBER>
::= A number containing a set of any of the following characters
0123456789_

<NUMBER>
Numbers can be specified in decimal, hexadecimal, octal or
binary, may optionally start with a + or -. The <BASE> token
controls what number digits are legal. <BASE> must be one of
d, h, o, or b, for the bases decimal, hexadecimal, octal and
binary respectively. A number can contain any set of the
following characters that is consistent with <BASE>:

0123456789abcdefABCDEFxXzZ?

<BASE> is one of the following tokens:
'b 'B 'o 'O 'd 'D 'h 'H

<concatenation>
::= { <expression> <,<expression>>* }

<multiple_concatenation>
::= { <expression> { <expression> <,<expression>>* } }

<function_call>
::= <name_of_function> (<expression> <,<expression>>*)
||= <name_of_system_function> (<expression>
    <,<expression>>*)
||= <name_of_system_function>

<name_of_system_function>
::= <SYSTEM_IDENTIFIER>

<SYSTEM_IDENTIFIER>
An <IDENTIFIER> that begins with a $. A SYSTEM_
IDENTIFIER cannot be escaped.

F.8   GENERAL

<identifier>

```
::= <IDENTIFIER><.<IDENTIFIER>>*
```

<IDENTIFIER>
>   An identifier is any sequence of letters, digits, dollar signs ($), and the underscore (_) symbol, except that the first must be a letter or the underscore; the first character may not be a digit or $. Upper and lower case letters are considered to be different. Escaped identifiers start with the backslash character (\) and may include any printable ASCII character. An escaped identifier ends with white space. The leading backslash character is not considered to be part of the identifier.

<delay>
```
::= # <number>                            Defined in SectionF.7.
| | = # <identifier>
| | = # ( <mintypmax_expression>
      <,<mintypmax_expression>>?
      <,<mintypmax_expression>>?)
```

<mintypmax_expression>   Defined in Section F.7.

<delay_control>
```
::= # <number>                            Defined in Section F.7.
| | = # <identifier>
| | = # ( <mintypmax_expression> )        Defined in Section F.7.
```

<event_control>
```
::= @ <identifier>
| | = @ ( <event_expression> )
```

<event_expression>
```
::= <expression>                          Defined in Section F.7.
| | = posedge <SCALAR_EVENT_EXPRESSION>
| | = negedge <SCALAR_EVENT_EXPRESSION>
| | = <event_expression> <or <event_expression>>*
```

<SCALAR_EVENT_EXPRESSION> is an expression that resolves to a one bit value.

Index